To
Gd

$ - 4 - 13

(handwritten signature) Ken Butterworth
Ac. 20 : 32

Plain Bible Talk

Ken Butterworth

Publishing Designs, Inc.

Publishing Designs, Inc.
P.O. Box 3241
Huntsville, Alabama 35810

Printed in the United States of America

Cover design: Crosslin Creative

Publisher's Cataloging-in-Publication Data

Butterworth, Ken, 1945—
Plain Bible Talk / Ken Butterworth.
Chapter questions
268 pp.
1. Bible Observations. 2. Topics of the Bible. 3. Christian conduct
ISBN : 978-0-929540-84-9
248.4

Contents

In Memory 5

Dedication 6

1. About God 7

2. About Bible Terminology 12

3. About Christ 17

4. About Biblical Authority 22

5. About Bible Study 27

6. About the One Blood-Bought Church 34

7. About Never Giving Up 39

8. About Alcohol, Drugs, and Tobacco 44

9. About Attendance 49

10. About "Apple of Eden" Doctrine 54

11. About the Lord's Supper 59

12. About Answering Our Families and Friends 64

13. About Right and Wrong 69

14. About the Blood-Stained Cross 74

15. About the Seriousness of Worship 79

16. About Instruments in Worship 84

17. About What Granny Would Have Said 89

18. About Satan's Hydrophobia 94

19. About Biblical Love 99

20. About the Importance of Names 103

21. About Being Stars for God 108

22. About Going Beyond What Is Written 113

23. About Human Suffering 118

24. About Why There Are So Many Churches 123

25. About the Religion of Islam 128

26. About Heaven 133

27. About Hell 138

28. About Beatitudes 143

29. About Gambling 148

30. About Seeking a New Way 153

31. About Prayer 158

32. About Hard Questions 163

33. About Immodesty 168

34. About John 3:16 173

35. About Preventing Church Problems 178

36. About the Rapture 183

37. About Rightly Dividing the Bible 189

38. About Evolution 194

39. About the Baptist Church 199

40. About Psalm 119 204

41. About Individual Responsibility 209

42. About the Perfect Plan of Redemption 214

43. About the Book of Revelation 218

44. About the Word *If* 223

45. About Teaching the Next Generation 227

46. About the Devil 232

47. About the Ten Commandments 237

48. About Responsibility and Excuse-Making 242

49. About Making Our Home a Christian Home 247

50. About Cemeteries, Graves, and Tombstones 253

51. About Gluttony 258

52. About Members of the Church of Christ 264

In Memory

With the publication of this volume, I sadly, lovingly, and affectionately honor the memory of our son Jack—Kenneth Eugene Butterworth II—who died on May 16, 2010. I struggle to put in words my (our) love for him. We miss him so much, and each day brings awful pain, sorrow, hurt, and anguish that torment our souls. Every day is filled with memories of yesteryear. His mother and I now know first hand the full, crushing, and horrible impact of a broken heart. I thank God for each sunrise, even though it is another day of feeling as if I have been buried alive. Jack was our firstborn, and provided us with a multitude of fond, happy, and loving times. Yes, precious memories, how they flood my soul. He loved his family, and adored his two children (our grandchildren). Jack and I never ended a phone conversation without telling each other, "I love you." We never parted without a hug and an "I love you."

As is usually the case, he loved his mother so very, very much. I confess that I never realized how a soul could be so intensely tormented day by day, until Jack died. I would not wish this heartache on anyone, and I pray that mothers and daddies everywhere will cherish each and every opportunity they have with their children, regardless of their ages. I implore all parents to seize the moment with the little ones they brought into the world, to hug, love, and teach them God's ways.

Our faith has never wavered one iota. Satan will not "beat" us, but Jack's mother and I know that we will never again know true peace in our earthly bodies. God is so good to us. He blessed us with three other children, four grandchildren, and two great-grandchildren. We are indeed blessed.

I pray this book will help many to a clearer understanding of what is really important. May we all realize that the only thing that really and truly matters is to die in the Lord.

Dedication

This book is affectionately, lovingly and respectfully dedicated to every brother, sister, and congregation who has encouraged me to write, and then supported me to do so. Without you, I could not have put these materials into book form. Thank you for doing your part for the Master's cause.

I especially appreciate the *Beaches* congregation in Mexico Beach, Florida. You may be small in number but you are known personally by heaven's hosts. You brethren are a great source of encouragement to me and my wife. With the exception of *my wife* and three precious friends in Birmingham, Alabama—*Elizabeth Brown, Jerry Monosky,* and *Gerri Monosky*—you brethren were the first to encourage me to write. Thank you! You are a faithful, dedicated, sweet, and determined congregation. When our heavenly Father allowed you to become a part of my life, it was indeed a special and unique blessing. I am a better person because of you. You have always made our heavenly Father proud, and you continue to serve the Master with respect and love. You are indeed a glory and honor to our heavenly Father, and I sincerely love, appreciate, and respect you so very much. Because of you, God is glorified, Christ is magnified, the cross is sanctified, and the church is alive and well in Gulf County, Florida. My prayer is that you brethren will never give up, give out, or give in. Stay the course, and God bless you allowing multitudes to know the ways of God.

Your Brother in Him,
Ken Butterworth

Acts 28:15
And from thence, when the brethren heard of us,
they came to meet us as far as Appii forum,
and The tree taverns; whom when Paul saw,
he thanked God, and took courage.

1

Plain Bible Talk

ABOUT GOD

PURPOSE
To maintain and strengthen our faith in the one true God (Isa. 45:21).

GOAL
To accept the fact that God does exist and He made it all (Ps. 19:1–3).

CHALLENGING THOUGHT
God made everything in six literal days (Gen. 1:1–31).

KEY WORDS

God	evolution	one
creation	atheism	inspiration

CHOICES BEFORE US
Either God exists or atheism and evolution are right.

THREE GREAT TRUTHS
There is a God in heaven (Dan. 2:28).
He is able to deliver (Dan. 3:17).
He rules in the kingdom of men (Dan. 4:25).

SCRIPTURES TO BE READ AND STUDIED

Genesis 1:1	Exodus 3:14
Ecclesiastes 12:13	Isaiah 44:8
Isaiah 45:5, 12, 18	Habakkuk 2:20
Acts 17:24	Ephesians 4:6

PRAYER FOR TODAY

Our heavenly Father, we acknowledge Thee as the one true, great God who created all things. We bow before Thee and give Thee praise for it all.

God, the Creator

To know anything about God we must know there is a God. He has always existed (Exod. 3:14). He is omnipotent (all powerful), omnipresent (everywhere), and omniscient (all knowing). He is the creator of everything (Isa. 45:5, 12, 18). He is great, good, holy, loving, just, and wrathful. He means what He says. He is longsuffering but He will not tolerate sin and immaturity forever. He cannot lie; He will always do right (Gen. 18:25). Simply put, God dictates the rules that govern His creation. That is the reason a potato will never produce a tomato and a fish will never produce a gorilla (Gen. 1:11–12).

What a great God we serve! (Ps. 95:3). While man can never fully explain God, he can proclaim Him. A failure to recognize that God is in control of His creation will cause man to depend on himself (Rom. 1:21). From our prospective, God sometimes delays in the fulfillment of His promises, but He will not deny us what we truly need. He created us, loves us, and knows what is best for us (Ps. 139:13–14).

Respecting God

The Bible—God's breathed words—sustains the fact that 5,972 years ago, as of 2013, God made it all (Gen. 1:1). Yes, I believe in the "big bang" theory. God said it and "BANG!" it happened. Everyone should believe there is a God, believe in Him, and believe what He says. God challenged the people in Isaiah's day to prove that He does not exist (Isa. 41:21). We should have the same mindset and put the infidel on the defensive! There is an abundance of proof concerning the existence of God. God laughs at man's futility in thinking that he has found a different and better way (Ps. 2:3–4; 37:13; 59:8). Man must fear, respect, and revere the God of heaven (Job 23:15–16). When man begins to make changes concerning the Bible, church, worship, creation, obedience, and such like, he is saying that his way is better than God's. One of the primary reasons the Bible was written is to prove the existence of God. Yes, God does exist and His holy and great name is due our respect (Ps. 111:9; Eccles. 12:13).

The Biggest Fool of All

Atheism says there is no God; pantheism says the whole universe is God; polytheism says there are many gods; deism says there is a supreme being but he does nothing for man; and agnosticism says the existence of God cannot be proved or disproved. All those who hold these philosophies are fools (Ps. 14:1; 53:1). There will be no atheists in hell, but all too-late confessors will be there (Phil. 2:10–11). As for me and my house, we will serve God (Josh. 24:15). Organic evolution can neither be proved in a laboratory nor demonstrated outside one (1 Cor. 3:19). Those involved in these "isms" will face God in judgment, and He will not let their unbeliefs slide (2 Thess. 1:7–10).

Proof That God Exists

Ten reasons for believing in God:
1. The Bible is based on His existence (Gen. 1:1).
2. Jesus proclaims this truth (Matt. 10:32–33; 19:4; 24:37–39; Mark 10:6), and we can know that Jesus lived among earthly creatures.
3. A denial of God is the only alternative to faith (Ps. 14:1).
4. Nature affirms God (Ps. 139:13–14).
5. The world about us is a witness for God (Rom. 1:20; Acts 14:17; 17:25).
6. Inspiration supports God's existence (2 Tim. 3:16–17; 2 Pet. 1:20–21).
7. Common reasoning affirms that God made all things (Job 38:1–4).
8. Science defends the reality of God and proves He is in control (Job 37:6; Isa. 40:22).
9. The universe confirms God's existence (Heb. 3:4; Ps. 102:25).

10. Morality proves God exists because sin violates His law (Eccles. 7:29). Did Hitler break the moral law of Germany, England, or the United States when he murdered thousands of Jews? No. He broke God's law!

A Challenge

Questions: If there is no God, then evolution is true. Is this what you affirm and believe? If so, have you ever seen a half man or half ape? Would such an animal have a half soul? Where would he get his half soul? Could he say half the alphabet? Who taught him? Would you please explain how woman and baby evolved? What was the bee before it became a bee? A pre-bee? Can you show us a fossil that depicts one animal changing into another? Can a living being come from non-living matter? Of course not! So prove your case. What new proof will you offer that God does not exist? (Isa. 41:21). Or could it just be that the Bible is true after all?

QUESTIONS

1. God has always _____ (Exod. 3:14).
2. One of the major reasons as to why the Bible was written is to prove the _____ of _____.
3. God is _____ (all powerful), _____ (everywhere) and _____ (all knowing).
4. _____ cannot be demonstrated or _____ (1 Cor. 3:19).
5. God challenged the people in _____ day to prove that He does not _____ (Isa. 41:21).
6. _____ says there is no God, _____ says the whole universe is God Himself, _____ says there are many gods, _____ says there is a supreme being, but he does nothing for man, and _____ says one cannot prove nor disprove God's existence.
7. God made everything in _____ literal _____ (Gen. 1:1-31).

8. There is a _____ in heaven (Dan. 2:28), He is _____ to _____ us (Dan. 3:17) and He _____ in the _____ of men (Dan. 4:25).
9. Man cannot _____ explain _____, but can proclaim Him.
10. God cannot _____ and will always do _____ (Gen. 18:25).

True or False

1. ____ There are times that God laughs at man. Give scriptural proof for your answer. _____
2. ____ Even though God created man, He does not know what is best for him. Give scriptural proof for your answer. _____
3. ____ Jesus proves that God exists. Give scriptural proof for your answer. _____
4. ____ There will be folks in hell who were atheists while on earth, but in hell there will be no atheists. Give scriptural proof for your answer. _____
5. ____ It is possible for a tomato to produce a potato. Give scriptural proof for your answer. _____

Five Simple Questions

1. How many "half man, half ape" sightings have been reported?
2. What was the bee before it evolved into a bee?
3. What evidence does the evolutionist have that horses grew taller so they could outrun tigers? What reason does he give for the tigers not growing taller—and faster—so they could catch the horses?
4. Where have fossils of animals in the process of changing from one kind to another been unearthed?
5. How can the evolutionist explain how woman and baby evolved?

2

Plain Bible Talk

ABOUT
BIBLE TERMINOLOGY

PURPOSE
To understand the eternal importance of using Bible language.

GOAL
To learn what God demands and requires concerning our speech.

CHALLENGING THOUGHT
In order to convert others, one must speak Bible language.

KEY WORDS

doctrine	speech	authority
corrupt	sound	

CHOICES BEFORE US
Either speak sound doctrine (use Bible language) or use the religious language of man.

THREE GREAT TRUTHS
A person is known by his speech.
Speech not based on God's teachings is corrupt.
God is pleased when one uses Bible language.

SCRIPTURES TO BE READ AND STUDIED

Judges 12:1–6	1 Peter 4:11
Matthew 12:37; 26:73	Romans 16:18
Titus 2:1	Nehemiah 13:23–24
Ephesians 4:29	Mark 12:37

PRAYER FOR TODAY

God, please give us the courage and determination to use Bible language. Help us always to speak Thy holy and divine truths.

Our Responsibility

Without an understandable language, one cannot know what is being taught (Gen. 11:1–9). That fact applies equally to spiritual matters. The Bible is the standard for all speech concerning religious matters. The English language has some 500,000 words in its vocabulary. There are some 773,746 words in the King James Version of the Bible. Surely one can find good and right words to use in everyday life. Just as Peter's speech revealed his identity, so will ours. As members of the blood-bought church, we are obligated to use Bible terminology. When we fail to do so, we then become just another denomination. The truth, including our speech, distinguishes us from all other religious groups. Living apart from the world means to speak Bible language (Gal. 4:30). If Christians do not use Bible language, the world will never hear it.

Our Obligation

Many Christians believe the church would be better served by the use of terminology that is acceptable to our religious friends, so some of our brethren are using a "weasel" language to fit in with the crowd. They are making a cardinal mistake. Their practice is costing the church dearly. When Christians use Bible talk, they are speaking sound doctrine (Tit. 2:1). Bible talk will lay a firm foundation on which to erect a spiritual building. We owe it to our neighbors to use Bible language.

Our Downfall

To ignore Bible terminology is to disrespect God and His Word, to fail to walk in the old paths (Jer. 6:16), and to create bypaths (Jer. 18:15).

The language of Ashdod is still with us (Neh. 13:23–24). Christians talk like the religions about them because they desire to please men (Luke 6:26; Gal. 1:10). Begin now to use language that is based on a "God said" premise. The church's failure to do so has led to liberalism that has resulted in many sinful changes concerning its purpose.

Our Examples

The world has influenced our everyday speech as well. If words and language do not mean anything, try shouting "Roll Tide" or "War Eagle" at a company picnic in Alabama. Playing cowboys and Indians has become playing "cow persons and native Americans." A used car is now a previously owned car. A "thuggy" thief is a home invader. Adultery is a fling or an affair. A drunk is a diseased being. Homosexuals are gay. A sinner is morally challenged.

Our examples should be found in the Bible, not in society. We have allowed society to desensitize us in sin's marketplace by renaming Satan's available products. We have swallowed the new vocabulary hook, line, and sinker. We are in dire need of plain and understandable language (John 11:14; 18:34). We do not need preachers who almost preach. We need preachers who will preach, those who will unequivocally state, "And God says."

Get a good dictionary and look up *golly, doggone, son of a gun, dad gum, god dog, shoot, and gee whiz.* Should these words ever come from the mouth of a Christian?

Our Hope, the Pattern of the Bible

1. Sunday is the first day of the week; it is not the Sabbath (Acts 20:7).
2. When an invitation is extended following a gospel message, it is an invitation to respond to the will of Christ, not to "pray through" at the altar (Acts 2:37–47).
3. When a person obeys the gospel, he neither joins the church nor is he voted into it. He is added to the Lord's church by the Lord (Acts 2:37–47).
4. A person obeys the gospel. He does not "accept Jesus as his personal savior" (Heb. 5:8–9, Acts 2:37–47).

5. Salvation requires obedient faith, not faith only (Rom. 1:5; James 2:24).

6. Christians give as they have been prospered on the first day of the week; they do not tithe (1 Cor. 16:1–2).

7. Faith is necessary in order to be saved, but no one is saved by faith only (Mark 16:16).

8. Preachers are not Reverends, Fathers, or Pastors (Ps. 111:9; Matt. 23:7–9; 1 Tim. 3:1–7).

9. The whole church is to sing during worship. Performances by choirs, trios, and soloists are devices of men for their own entertainment (Eph. 5:17–19).

10. The one blood-bought church was paid for with the blood of Christ, and it should not wear a denominational name such as Methodist, Baptist, or Presbyterian (Rom. 16:16; 1 Cor. 1:13).

QUESTIONS

1. Without an _____ language, one cannot know what is being _____.
2. The _____ is the standard for all _____ concerning _____ matters.
3. As members of the _____ _____ _____, we are obligated to use _____ _____.
4. Far too many want to just "_____ _____" with the crowd.
5. To ignore _____ _____ is to disrespect _____ and His _____.
6. We have allowed _____ to desensitize us in sin's marketplace by _____ Satan's available products.
7. We do not need preachers who will _____ _____.
8. One will speak either _____ doctrine (Bible language) or the religious _____ of man.
9. We are in dire need of _____ and _____ language.
10. The truth (including our speech) distinguishes us from all other _____ _____.

TRUE OR FALSE

1. ____ Sunday is the seventh day of the week.
2. ____ Gospel preachers are not to be called Reverend, Pastor, or Father.
3. ____ The one blood-bought church can be called by whatever name man so chooses.
4. ____ Christians "tithe" on the first day of the week.
5. ____ One must have obedient faith; not faith only.

FIVE SIMPLE QUESTIONS

1. What scripture commands us to "speak sound doctrine"?
2. What do some now call a sinner?
3. What special words are now used instead of adultery?
4. What does God call a man who is called a "diseased person" in today's society?
5. What is a cowardly way to speak called?

3

Plain Bible Talk

ABOUT CHRIST

PURPOSE
To know assuredly that Jesus is the Christ, the only begotten Son of God.

GOAL
To learn more about our Savior and His mission.

CHALLENGING THOUGHT
Jesus, the Son of God, actually and literally lived on this earth.

KEY WORDS

Christ	Jesus	Immanuel
King	Savior	Redeemer
Friend	Judge	

CHOICES BEFORE US
Either Jesus is who He claims to be or the Bible has promoted one of the biggest lies ever.

THREE GREAT TRUTHS
Jesus has always existed.
He was resurrected on the third day.
He is coming again.

SCRIPTURES TO BE READ AND STUDIED

Genesis 3:1	Isaiah 7:14
Galatians 4:4	Matthew 1:21; 17:5

PRAYER FOR TODAY
Father, we thank Thee for Thy Son and our Savior, in whom Thy love was exemplified and magnified. We thank Thee for Jesus and for His love for us.

Some Things the Bible Does Not Reveal

God chose not to reveal certain things to us (Deut. 29:29). Examples: Whether or not Adam had a belly button. The day of Christ's second coming (Matt. 24:36). What Jesus looked like. (No picture or portrait was ever made of Him.) What He wrote on the ground (John 8:8). The month and day of His birth. ("Bishop" Liberius, in AD 354, set December 25 as the date for Christ's birth. God did not reveal such!) Jesus should be viewed as the risen Savior, not a babe in a manger. His birth would not have mattered had He not gone to the cross, been buried, and been resurrected on the third day (1 Cor. 15:1–4). To celebrate December 25 as the date of Christ's birth is to ignore God's word and accept man's (Gal. 4:9–10). Who is your authority? Liberius or God? What saith the scripture? (Acts 5:29; Gal. 4:30).

Some Things the Bible Reveals

Only forty days in the life of Christ are mentioned in the Bible and only eight of those days are detailed, yet He changed the world forever! Some teach that there was a "pre-existence" of Christ, but there has never been a time He has not existed (Gen. 1:26; John 1:1, 14; Col. 1:15–16). (He, of course, having existed eternally, pre-existed His incarnate or fleshly form.) From the promise in Genesis 3:15 till His birth, 3,959 years elapsed before the right time came for His birth (Gal. 4:4). The singular theme of all the Bible is "the coming of Christ." Every event, nation, and character was a part of God's masterful plan for the Lord's coming. There are some 333 prophecies of Christ recorded in the Old Testament, and all of them came to pass. His mission was to save the lost (Matt. 1:21; Luke 19:10). That salvation was made possible by His death and resurrection.

We should always remember six things Jesus has done for us.

1. He loved us when we did not deserve it.
2. He has forgiven His obedient children of their sins.

3. He has given us a purpose and a plan for our lives.

4. He has given us peace of mind.

5. He is our ever constant companion.

6. He has prepared our eternal home.

Yes, I believe in the one they call Jesus, and God has revealed everything He wanted us to know about Him (2 Peter 1:3–4).

Some Specific Things Revealed about Christ

1. He is God's only begotten Son (John 3:16).
2. His birth was prophesied (Gen. 3:15).
3. His death was prophesied (Isa. 53).
4. His resurrection was prophesied (Ps. 16:10).
5. He was born of a virgin (Matt. 1:23).
6. He was a Jew (Matt. 1:1–25).
7. He was a carpenter (Mark 6:3).
8. He was no anemic weakling as often displayed by drawings (Matt. 21:12–13; John 2:13–16).
9. He was not especially handsome (Isa. 53:2).
10. He apparently had a beard (Isa. 50:6).
11. He did not have a place of His own to lay His head (Matt. 8:20).
12. He was born in Bethlehem (Matt. 2:1).
13. He was carried to Egypt at age two to avoid death (Matt. 2:13–16).
14. He was obedient to His parents (Luke 2:51).
15. He was busy for God at age twelve (Luke 2:41–49).
16. He was baptized at age thirty (Luke 3:23).
17. He was crucified three years later at Calvary (Matt. 27).
18. He was a cousin to John the Baptist, who was six months older than He (Luke 1:26–37).
19. His death is detailed in all four of the Gospel accounts.
20. He was resurrected the third day and ascended to heaven forty days later (Acts 1:1–11).
21. He is coming again (2 Thess. 1:7–9).
22. He will be our judge (Acts 17:30–31).

23. He is now at the right hand of God, reigning on His throne (Acts 2:29–34).
24. He is the head, founder, and savior of the church (Col. 1:18; Matt. 16:18; Eph. 5:23).

One Precious and Specific Thing That Is Revealed

Jesus shed His blood—all His blood—to purchase the church (Acts 20:28). Not a single drop of His blood was for the purchase of even one denomination! There is not one denomination that has the scriptural right to exist, not one! The church of Christ—say it, brethren!—is the one and only church for which our Lord died (Rom. 16:16). He shed His blood for all who have lived, are living, and shall live (Isa. 53:6; Rom. 5:8). But please note that He will bear the sins of many—not everyone (Isa. 53:12). Is this a contradiction? No, because even though He died for all, He will bear the sins of only those who obey Him (Heb. 5:8–9). To obey Him, follow the teachings of Romans 10:17; John 8:24; Luke 13:3; Romans 10:9–10; and Acts 2:38.

What a Savior! What a God we serve! What a church we are privileged to be members of! What a book—the Bible—we have as a guide! What a hope we have in heaven!

QUESTIONS

1. God chose not to _____ certain things to _____.
2. "_____" _____ set December 25 as the _____ for Christ's birth.
3. The singular theme of all the Bible is the "_____ ___ _____."
4. His mission was to _____ the lost.
5. He (Jesus) is the _____, _____ and _____ of the church.
6. Jesus shed _____ _____ (all of His _____) to purchase the _____.
7. There are some 333 prophecies of _____ under the _____ _____ and all of them came to _____.
8. Not a single drop of His _____ was for the purchase of even _____ _____!
9. What a _____ (Bible) we have as a _____!
10. The church of _____ (say it brethren!) is the _____ and only _____ for which our Lord _____.

TRUE OR FALSE

1, ____ Jesus has always existed.
2. ____ The Bible confirms December 25 as the birthday of Christ.
3. ____ We know exactly what Jesus looked like.
4. ____ Only forty days of the life of Christ are mentioned in the Bible.
5. ____ Jesus was twelve years old when He was baptized.

FIVE SIMPLE QUESTIONS

1. Who was Jesus' cousin?
2. What two verses state that Jesus is the head of the church (body)?
3. What verse states that Jesus was a carpenter?
4. How many years elapsed between Genesis 3:15–16 and Matthew 1:21?
5. What Old Testament scripture prophesied that Jesus would be born of a virgin?

4

Plain Bible Talk

ABOUT BIBLICAL AUTHORITY

PURPOSE
To know that the Bible is the one and only source of authority for all spiritual things.

GOAL
To accept the Bible as God's Word, never tampering with it.

CHALLENGING THOUGHT
What God says settles the matter, whether we believe it or not.

KEY WORDS
authority	Bible	revelation
inspiration	standard	scriptures

CHOICES BEFORE US
Either the Bible is God's breathed words or it is a fake.

THREE GREAT TRUTHS
The Bible is right on every subject it addresses.
The Bible is never out of date.
The Bible is what it claims to be, the breathed words of God.

SCRIPTURES TO BE READ AND STUDIED
Psalm 119:89, 128	Psalm 119:160–161
Proverbs 30:6	2 Timothy 2:15; 3:16–17
Revelation 22:18–19	2 John 9–11

PRAYER FOR TODAY
Our Father, we give Thee thanks for Thine inspired and perfect Word.

Introduction

When the following article came across my desk, I carefully filed it because it revealed a sad state of affairs within the Lord's church. We create an eternal tragedy when we fail to indoctrinate the next generation! The article summarizes the result of a survey by one of our "Christian" universities. Five hundred young people (ages 11–19) in churches of Christ were asked about their beliefs. (Percentages indicate agreement.)

- Church membership does not matter as long as you love God (65%).
- One must be an active member of the church to go to heaven (14%).
- Adultery is the only biblical reason for divorce (39%).
- Christians should be very different from the world in dress, language, and general conduct (31%).
- Using instruments in worship is sinful (10%).
- It is wrong for girls to lead youth group devotions or singings (11%).
- Women should never take a leadership role in worship (22%).
- Christians should avoid any and all alcoholic beverages (32%).
- Abortion is wrong (66%).
- God will punish the wicked in a literal hell (79%).
- Nations who do not hear about Jesus have no hope for salvation (22%).

We have failed in teaching our youth the importance of biblical authority! It is little wonder the church is drifting!

The Bible Must Be Our First and Last Source of Authority
The Bible is never outdated (Ps. 119:89; Matt. 24:35). It has the right answer on every subject it addresses (Ps. 119:128). We must form the habit of asking, "What saith the scriptures?" (Gal. 4:30). The Bible is the one, true standard and rule book (Phil. 3:16). It is the only inspired source of authority (2 Tim. 3:16–17; 2 Pet. 1:3; John 12:48). God actually and literally breathed the words of the Bible (2 Tim. 3:16–17). Human creeds are divisive and create man-made churches (1 Cor. 1:10). It is a sin not to know the Bible (Matt. 22:29); everyone must hear it (Jer. 22:29). The chain of authority is God, Christ, the Holy Spirit, the apostles, and the written Word. Yes, the Bible—not feelings, conscience, visions, common sense, human creeds, Mom, Dad, or the preacher—is the source of authority.

The Bible Is from God
The Bible is verbally and completely inspired, the breathed words of God, so it is not only logical but it is always right. The Bible reveals God, guides us, answers every question of man, and tells us about sin. God Himself is the author (2 Pet. 1:3) and, therefore, not a single contradiction can be found upon its pages.

The Bible has been confirmed by history, prophecy, archaeology, science, and chronology. More than five thousand manuscripts and partial manuscripts of the Bible have been found. The Bible has been attacked by every means, and yet no one has proved it is not from God (Ps. 12:6).

It is indestructible! *Bible* comes from *biblion* meaning book, roll, scroll. The word *Bible*, meaning the entirety of God's revelation, does not appear in Holy Writ.

Man Did Not Write the Bible of His Own Efforts
No man inserted his opinions, likes, or dislikes upon the pages of Holy Writ. Had man written the Bible, there would be some things left out. Atheists would never have written Psalm 14:1. Liberals would not have inserted 1 Corinthians 4:6 and 2 John 9–11. Denominational boards would not have written Acts 2:38 or 1 Corinthians 1:10. Universalists, who believe everyone will be saved, most certainly did not write Hebrews 5:8–9. Modern day "sissy" preachers would not have penned 2 Timothy

4:2. The immoral would not have allowed Matthew 19:1–9. The "church changers" would never have written Romans 16:16. God put His words in men's mouths and those men in turn wrote those words down (Jer. 1:9; 2 Pet. 1:20–21; Rev. 1:11).

The Bible Is God's Unique Book

There will never be another book like the Bible (Jude 3). God commands us to rightly divide His word (2 Tim. 2:15). Its message can and must be consistent with itself, else God lied (Rev. 1:3). The Bible is simple and understandable (2 Tim. 3:15). It is a sacred and holy book (2 Tim. 3:15). It is knowable (2 Tim. 3:14–15). It is profitable for study (2 Tim. 3:16). It produces faith (2 Tim. 3:15). It makes one wise (2 Tim. 3:15). It will judge us (John 12:48).

Begin now to read and study the Bible; its message will deepen your faith. What God says is the foundation for everything. Ask for, demand, and give Bible proof for all you do. The Bible is the foundation of it all, and our attitude toward the Bible is our attitude toward God.

QUESTIONS

1. The Bible is what it claims to _____, the _____ _____ of God.
2. It is an _____ tragedy when we fail to _____ the next _____.
3. We have failed in teaching our _____ the importance of _____ _____.
4. The Bible must be our _____ and last source of _____.
5. The "chain" of authority is _____, _____, _____ _____, _____ and the written _____.
6. The Bible has been confirmed by _____, _____, _____, _____ and _____.
7. The word "Bible" means _____ or the _____.
8. God commands us to rightly _____ His word.
9. Human creeds are _____ and create man-made _____.
10. _____ would never have written Psalm 14:1.

TRUE OR FALSE

1. ____ Five thousand, three hundred manuscripts of the Bible have been found.
2. ____ God put His words in men's mouths and they wrote down those words.
3. ____ The Bible sometimes contradicts itself.
4. ____ The Bible has the right answer on every subject.
5. ____ The Bible becomes "outdated" and must be revised from time to time.

FIVE SIMPLE QUESTIONS

1. What does God think of those who do not know the Bible?
2. Who would not have written 2 Timothy 4:2?
3. What will deepen one's faith?
4. When God says something, why does that settle the matter?
5. What verse proves that the Bible is simple and knowable?

5

Plain Bible Talk

ABOUT BIBLE STUDY

PURPOSE
To suggest a guideline for studying the Bible so it can be rightly divided.

GOAL
To remind everyone that God intended for the Bible to be understood.

CHALLENGING THOUGHT
The way we treat the Bible is the way we treat God.

KEY WORDS
study	patience	prayer
growth	ignorance	

CHOICES BEFORE US
Either we study the Bible and gain faith or we remain in ignorance.

THREE GREAT TRUTHS
The Bible was written to be understood.
We must rightly divide the Bible.
All can understand the Bible so we can all see it alike.

SCRIPTURES TO BE READ AND STUDIED
2 Timothy 2:15	2 Peter 3:18
Hosea 4:6	2 Chronicles 34:21

PRAYER FOR TODAY
*O Jehovah, give us wisdom as we meditate upon Thy
holy book.*

Introduction

A daily study—not just a reading!—of the Bible is imperative if one is to grow in Christ (2 Pet. 3:18). Jesus told the Sadducees they erred "not knowing the scriptures" (Matt. 22:29). The only way to know God is to know His book and to allow it to control us. In order for us to develop spiritually, we must study (1 Pet. 2:2; Heb. 5:12; 6:2). Always consider Bible study a privilege, not a chore. Allow it to be a desire, not a duty. Many who want to know the Bible do not know how to study it. Thus, the outline herein is presented to that end. Five simple steps to gain a knowledge of the Bible: study, study, study, study, and then study some more!

Many Do Not Know How to Study the Bible

Many have no concern for God's wishes. They prefer to cater to people and accumulate things which lead to spiritual ignorance (Mark 4:19). Some simply do not know how to study! Here are some suggestions.

Pulpit Preaching Alone Will Not Get You to Heaven

Why do so many people depend on a preacher to tell them what to believe?

- "The preacher is God's spokesman. I must listen to him."
- "The more I know, the more I'm accountable for."
- "I have neither the time nor energy to make an in-depth study of the Bible."
- "I know enough about the Bible already."
- "We can make the Bible mean anything we want it to."
- "If I took the Bible at face value, I would have to believe many of my friends are lost."
- "The Bible is a great book, but it is not to be followed literally."

Why Do Some Attempt to Study and Yet Fall Short?

- They do not study "smartly."
- They do not take all the Bible says on a subject.

- They worry over what the Bible does not say.
- They study "about" the Bible and do not study the Bible itself.
- They study just enough to become confused.

Suggestions for Studying the Bible

1. Set a time for daily Bible study and stick rigidly to that schedule.
2. Approach Bible study as a good investment. Knowledge is not without a price!
3. Respect the Bible and study it in view of a better life. God wrote it for you and His words will judge you. The Bible is right on every subject it addresses.
4. Begin every study with a prayer and allow God's Word to increase your knowledge and wisdom.
5. Use the King James Version or the American Standard Version in your regular study. Other translations may be useful for reference.
6. Take your Bible to worship and to Bible classes. Preachers and teachers are not inspired, so listen, read, and study as they teach.
7. Study passages in their contexts. For example, the law of Moses was still in effect when Jesus and His disciples observed the Old Testament Passover feast, at which time He instituted the Lord's supper (Matt. 26:18–29). Never take scriptures out of context to prove your beliefs.
8. Determine the author, the date, and the audience of the scripture you are studying when possible. These facts will greatly help you to understand the message.
9. View the Bible as the fundamental and authoritative source for preaching, religion, living, judgment, faith, worship, creation, prophecy, inspiration, and the revealed Word. Keep this in mind and your Bible study efforts will be more productive.
10. Study to learn the ways of God, not to prove someone or some religious doctrine wrong. While error must be dealt with, do not allow that motive to become your reason for and approach to Bible study.
11. Add good reference books to your library: Bible dictionary, concordance, atlas, and a set of Bible encyclopedias.

12. Select a good commentary with care. Even the best are written from man's point of view.

13. Remember that pulpit preaching alone will not get you to heaven (2 Tim. 2:15; 2 Pet. 3:18).

14. Plan a long-range study, such as a study of the prophets, specific chapters, and selected books. Then plan a short-range study, such as this material and other general and basic biblical information.

15. Search out good church bulletins and brotherhood publications. Study and then study some more. One never graduates from Bible study until he meets the Author face to face! Now is the time to develop the habit of studying the Bible. Your soul and the church's future depend on it.

16. Watch your faith grow as you become closer to God.

Here are a few points that will help you to study.
- The Old Testament lays the foundation for the work of Christ.
- Matthew, Mark, Luke, and John tell of the coming of Christ.
- Acts provides a history of men and women coming into Christ.
- Romans through Jude emphasizes continuing in Christ.
- Revelation tells of Christians being crowned in Christ.

A Simple Outline of the Bible

1. *The creation* (Gen. 1–5). Time covered is 1,656 years, 3859–2304 BC. The theme is the creation.

2. *The universal flood* (Gen. 6:1–11:26). Time covered is 427 years, 2304–1877 BC. The theme is sin, fall of man, and the flood.

3. *The patriarchs* (Gen. 11:27–50:26). Time covered is 215 years, 1877–1662 BC. The theme is the lives of the patriarchs: Abraham, Isaac, and Jacob. The book of Job should be studied in this time period.

4. *The Egyptian bondage* (Gen. 42:1–Exod. 12:36). The time covered is 215 years, 1662–1447 BC. The theme is Hebrew bondage in Egypt and their freedom.

5. *The wilderness wandering* (Exod. 12:37–Deut. 34:12). Time covered is 40 years, 1447–1407 BC. The theme is their journey from Egypt to the land of Canaan.

6. *Entering Canaan* (Book of Joshua). The time covered is 7 years, 1407–1399 BC. The theme is their entrance into and the dividing of the land of Canaan among the tribes of Israel.

7. *The time of the judges* (Judges 1:1–1 Sam 8:22). The time covered is 350 years, 1399–1050 BC. The theme is the story of Israel in the land of Canaan.

8. *The united kingdom* (1 Sam. 9–1 Kings 11; 1 Chron. 1:1–2 Chron. 11:23). The time covered is 120 years, 1050–930 BC. The theme is the history of Israel as a united nation. Saul, David, and Solomon each ruled 40 years. Psalms, Proverbs, Ecclesiastes, and Song of Solomon should be studied in this time period.

9. *The divided kingdoms* (1 Kings 12:1–2 Kings 25:30; 2 Chron. 10–35). The time covered is 344 years, 930–586 BC. The theme is the history of the division of God's people and why they divided. God sent prophets into Israel and Judah (2 Kings 17:13–14). The 17 prophetic books should be read here. The prophets in chronological order: Obadiah (844 BC), Joel (830 BC), Jonah (785 BC), Amos (760 BC), Hosea (760–722 BC), Isaiah (740–686 BC), Micah (735–716 BC.), Nahum (660 BC), Zephaniah (632–627 BC), Jeremiah (627–585 BC), Lamentations (585 BC), Habakkuk (605 BC), Daniel (605–536 BC), Ezekiel (597–570 BC), Haggai (520 BC), Zechariah (520–518 BC), Ezra 1–6 (539–515 BC). Esther (485–465 BC), Ezra 7–10 (457 BC), Malachi (431–430 BC), and Nehemiah (444–418 BC). Notice that the events in Esther fall between Ezra 6 and 7.

10. *The captivity* (2 Kings 24–25; 2 Chron. 36). The time covered is 70 years, 605–539 BC. The theme is Judah's captivity. Israel, the 10 tribes of the northern kingdom, had been conquered by the Assyrians in 721 BC (2 Kings 17:1–5, 24–29). Those who remained in Palestine interbred with foreigners and produced the Samaritans of Jesus' day.

11. *The return from captivity* (Covered by Ezra, Nehemiah, Esther, Haggai, Zechariah. and Malachi). The time covered is 107 years, 529–431 BC. The theme is the history of the Jews going back home to rebuild the temple, Jerusalem, its walls, and to restore the law.

12. *The "400 silent years"* (Dan. 7–12). The time covered is roughly 400 years, 431 BC–AD 1. The theme is the history of the Jews from their return to the coming of Christ.

13. *The time of Christ* (Matt. 1–Acts 1). The time covered is 33 years, AD 1–33. The theme is the birth, life, work, death, burial, resurrection, and ascension of Christ.

14. *The church* (Acts 2:1–Rev. 22:27). The time covered is 63 years (AD 33–96). The theme is the establishment and growth of the church of Christ.

QUESTIONS

1. The only way to know _____ is to know His _____, and then allow it to _____ our minds.
2. Always consider Bible _____ a privilege, not a _____.
3. Many look to the _____ or _____ for their source of authority.
4. We can make the _____ mean anything we want it to.
5. Knowledge is not without_____.
6. Always ascertain the _____, _____, _____ of the scripture you are studying when possible.
7. Select a good _____ with care.
8. In order for us to develop_____, we must study.
9. Again, _____ _____ alone will not get you to heaven.
10. Five simple steps to gain a knowledge of the Bible: _____, _____, _____, _____, and then _____ some more!

TRUE OR FALSE

1. ____ The way we treat the Bible is the way we treat God.
2. ____ Studying about the Bible is not the same as studying the Bible itself.
3. ____ It is not necessary or beneficial to study the Bible daily.
4. ____ The Saul in the book of 1 Samuel is the same as the Saul in Acts 9.
5. ____ The Bible was written to be understood.

FIVE SIMPLE QUESTIONS

1. What verse says one errs (sins) by not knowing the scriptures?
2. Should one study the Bible for the sole purpose of proving someone wrong?
3. What book is right on every subject it addresses?
4. Is the Bible for everyone or just for preachers?
5. What is an example of a long range study? Short range?

6

Plain Bible Talk

ABOUT THE ONE BLOOD-BOUGHT CHURCH

PURPOSE
To reveal the church that Jesus purchased with His shed blood.

GOAL
To identify the one blood-bought church for which our Lord died.

CHALLENGING THOUGHT
There is but one true New Testament church.

KEY WORDS

church	one	organization
place	time	admission
name	worship	

CHOICES BEFORE US
Either Jesus died for only one church or He lied.

THREE GREAT TRUTHS
Jesus built His church.
There is but one blood-bought church.
The true church belongs to Christ.

SCRIPTURES TO BE READ AND STUDIED

Daniel 2:44	Isaiah 2:1–4
Matthew 16:18	Acts 2:37–47; 20:28
Romans 16:16	Eph. 1:22–23; 3:9–11; 4:4–6; 5:23

PRAYER FOR TODAY
Dear God, how we thank Thee for the one church of the Bible.

Introduction

Why am I a member of the church of Christ? I read about it in the Bible (Rom. 16:16), and there is no better answer. The church for which our Lord died is not mine, yours, or ours. It is the Lord's! Nowhere in the pages of Holy Writ does anyone read about choosing the church of his choice. Neither does God sanction the choosing of names, ways to worship Him, doctrines, or how to be saved. No man started the church of Christ. No, not even Alexander Campbell. Campbell did not come to America until 1809 and churches of Christ were already here. Congregations had been established in Bridgeport, Alabama, and Celina, Tennessee, as well as other places. When you find Christ's church, you find the one true church of the Bible because it was purchased with all the blood of Christ (Acts 20:28). Jesus is its head (Col. 1:18). Jesus is its savior (Eph. 5:23). Jesus died for it (Eph. 1:22–23, 4:4).

That One Church Can Be Identified

Many teach that no one can possibly identify that one church since there are so many churches in existence. If this is true, then God is a liar (Matt. 16:18; Acts 2:47), no one can be saved (Acts 2:37–47; Eph. 5:23), and God cannot be glorified (Eph. 3:21), God's spiritual family cannot be identified (1 Tim. 3:15), the kingdom cannot be identified, and we cannot identify our King (Col. 1:13; 1 Tim. 6:15). How sad!

The One Church Was in the Eternal Plan of God

That one church is the kingdom that the prophets revealed (Dan. 2:44; Isa. 2:1–4). God set His plan in motion and called His people out of the world into the church (Eph. 3:9–12). Is it possible to find that church? Yes, by searching the Scriptures, it can be identified.

The church:

- Is identified as Christ's church (Rom. 16:16).
- Is ruled by one and only one book—the Bible (Phil. 3:16).
- Is teaching the oracles of God (1 Pet. 4:11).

- Is directed by Christ as its head (Col. 1:18).
- Is guided in worship according to the Bible (John 4:24).
- Is united on the basis of biblical teaching (1 Cor. 1:10; 2 John 9–11).
- Is saved through obedience to God (Acts 2:37–47).
- Is not a denomination (Acts 20:28).
- Is scriptural in organization (Phil. 1:1).
- Is preparing a people for heaven (1 Thess. 4:13–17).

Yes, that church must be sought, identified, and entered before one can be saved (Eph. 5:23).

Can One Be Sure He Has Found That Church?

1. *It can be identified by its allegiance to its founder* (Matt. 16:18; Acts 20:28; 4:12). When one finds the church that claims Jesus as its sole founder and is authorized by Him, he has found that one blood-bought church.

2. *It can be identified by the place of its origin* (Isa. 2:2–3). That church is God's spiritual house (1 Tim. 3:15). The apostles would preach repentance, remission of sins (Luke 24:46–47), and wait in Jerusalem for the promise to come upon them (Acts 1:4). Thus, in the city of Jerusalem, the church became a reality (Acts 2:1, 38, 47).

3. *It can be identified by the time it was established* (Dan. 2:31–44). Old Testament prophesy said it would be established in the days of the Roman kings. That church was established in AD 33 while these kings ruled (Luke 2:1).

4. *It can be identified by its organization* (Phil. 1:1; 1 Tim. 3:1–7, 8–13).

5. *It can be identified by its worship* (John 4:23–24)—singing (Eph. 5:19), praying (Acts 2:42), partaking of the Lord's supper every Sunday (Matt. 26:26–28; Acts 20:7), giving (1 Cor. 16:1–2), and teaching God's Word (Acts 2:42; 20:7). When one finds the church that worships every Sunday through these five avenues, he has found that one blood-bought church of the Bible.

God Made It Plain

God allowed the church to be established at the right time (Gal. 4:4). That church can and must be identified in order to be saved. Thanks be unto our heavenly Father that we can identify it. All who will hear (Rom. 10:9–10), believe (John 8:24), repent (Luke 13:3), confess (Matt. 10:32–33), and be baptized (Acts 2:38) are saved and added to the one blood-bought church of the Bible (Acts 2:47). Jesus will save these faithful ones (Eph. 5:23).

What about the Many "Fine Churches"?

That oft-asked question is intended to promote division in Christianity, but who says denominational churches are fine? God or man? Choosing the church of your choice is the same as choosing the God, Lord, or Spirit of your choice. The Bible says there is only one each of these (Eph. 4:4–6). Why was the one church Jesus purchased with all His blood not good enough? Why did we need a thousand more or a hundred more? Why did we need even one more? There is no biblical authority for any others to exist (Col. 3:17). As for me and my house, we choose the one blood-bought church of the Bible, the church of Christ. What is your decision?

QUESTIONS

1. There is but _____ _____ New Testament _____.
2. I am a member of the church of Christ because I can _____ about it in the _____ in the Bible (Rom. 16:16).
3. Nowhere upon the _____ of holy _____ does anyone read about _____ the _____ of his choice.
4. That one church is the _____ that the _____ revealed.
5. When one finds the _____ that is authorized by _____, he has found that one _____ bought church.
6. The church is _____ _____ (1 Tim. 3:15).
7. Yes, that church must be _____, _____ and _____ before one can be saved (Eph. 5:23).
8. All who will _____ (Rom. 10:10), _____ (John 8:24), _____ (Luke 13:3), _____ (Matt. 10:32-33) and be _____ (Acts 2:38) are added to the ____ blood-bought church of the _____ (Acts 2:47).
9. Choosing the church of your choice is the same as choosing the _____, _____ or _____ of your choice.
10. As for me and my house, we choose the _____ _____ _____ church of the Bible, the _____ of _____.

TRUE OR FALSE

1. ____ Alexander Campbell started (founded) the church of Christ.
2. ____ Jesus is the head and savior of the church of Christ.
3. ____ The one and only rule book for the church must be the Bible.
4. ____ The church of Christ was founded in Germany in AD 1729.
5. ____ Jesus purchased the church with all of His blood.

FIVE SIMPLE QUESTIONS

1. Jesus died for how many churches?
2. In what city, in the year AD 33, was the church founded?
3. God commands what five avenues of worship on Sunday?
4. Where is Bible authority for man-made churches to exist?
5. If the one church (kingdom) cannot be identified, then how can a person identity Jesus as king over the kingdom? (1 Tim. 6:15).

7

Plain Bible Talk

ABOUT NEVER GIVING UP

PURPOSE
To challenge everyone never to give up.

GOAL
To discuss and present a guide that will encourage everyone never to give up.

CHALLENGING THOUGHT
God does not want anyone to give up.

KEY WORDS

steadfast	self-pity	selfish
burdens	hope	discouragement
determined		

CHOICES BEFORE US
One will determine either to continue or give up, give out, and give in.

THREE GREAT TRUTHS
God is always with us.
We with God are in the majority.
God cannot use a discouraged person.

SCRIPTURES TO BE READ AND STUDIED

Job 2:9–11; 13:15	1 Corinthians 15:58
Luke 9:62	Revelation 2:10

PRAYER FOR TODAY
Dear God, give us courage and determination to continue till the end.

Introduction

"Don't die on third" is an old saying in baseball. In other words, whatever it takes, make it home. How much more so in life! The only thing that really matters is to die in the Lord (Rev. 14:13). The man who discovered ancient Nineveh did so with almost the first shovel of dirt. The explorer before him had labored for months but stopped too soon. All the *ifs*, *ands*, and *buts* will not change the fact that many stop too soon. We should contend (Jude 3), continue trying (Rev. 3:2), get up and get to work (Heb. 12:12), be encouraged (Acts 28:15), and not allow anything to stop us (Rom. 8:31–39). So never give up. Don't die on third or you will lose it all.

Examples

Some of Jesus' disciples gave up (Luke 9:62). Some in Jesus' audience abandoned Him (John 6:60–66). Demas gave up (2 Tim. 4:10). Peter implied that others were giving up (2 Pet. 2:20–22). Folks are still giving up. Often in that number are the sick, the bereaved, the poor, the downtrodden, the handicapped, the selfish, and the covetous. Neither the devil nor any person "made" them give up. They chose to throw in the towel. Yes, we do have compassion for some of these misfortunate ones, but giving up is not the answer. Don't ever give up!

Caution! Some Things Are Discouraging

Everything in life and each new day are not always "the top of the morning." Maintain the attitude of "why me, Lord?" not in self-pity, but in awe: "Why have You been so good to me, Lord? What have I done to deserve the spiritual and material blessings You have heaped on me?" (We did get up this morning, didn't we?)

What are some things that can be discouraging? Our sinful nation, humanism, selfishness, the rot on TV, "barnyard" morals throughout society, the lack of discipline in the home, church, and society, the disrespect for the Bible, and the bruising and hurting of the church of Christ by liberals. Do not allow these things to drag you down, corrupt your minds, and stop your spiritual progress. God is not pleased with a discouraged person!

What Can We Do about These Things?

When our lives are teetering on the brink of despair, where can we find help? What is our main source? Fellow Christians? Yes, of course! We can turn to the church for solace. We can pray about these matters and ask others to pray for them also. We can learn of others' needs and lend our support. We can remember that there is a way of escape (1 Cor. 10:13). We can remember that with God the future is bright and we are never alone. We can look for God's blessings and become more able to bear our burdens. We can remind ourselves that we are not useless, that God created us for His service. We can remember to refuse self-pity, for when it engulfs us, Satan is victorious (Jonah 4:1–11).

Never Give Up on These

1. *God.* He may delay, but He will not deny His children. To whom will you turn if you give up on God? Believe, respect, and obey Him. He is the great God (Ps. 95:3); He is the only God (Isa. 45:5, 12, 18). He is in control; He hears your prayers and sees your tears (Isa. 38:5).

2. *The church.* Jesus did not establish His church to hurt anyone! The church should be a little bit of heaven on earth. If you give up on the one church, who can help you? No one! Have congregational pride. Love and pray for the church. Work with and for the church. Support it and put it first (Matt. 6:33). Misery awaits those who give up and forsake the church.

3. *Prayer.* This should be our first and last resort (1 Thess. 5:17). Prayer is powerful; prayer changes things. Prayer is mentioned some twenty-five times in connection with Christ's life. Not counting the book of Psalms, there are some 650 prayers in the Bible.

4. *Our nation.* With all of America's faults, it is still the greatest nation on earth. Compared to the rest of the world, we are exceedingly blessed, and we must use these blessings as springboards to teach the lost. A great nation will turn to and honor God and the

Bible (Ps. 33:12). Love this nation and our flag, and pray for our future. If you give up on our nation, where will you go? The flag burners should be shipped out of this country!

5. *Your mate.* It is sad that many married couples spend valuable time arguing, fussing, and bickering. We have only a few short years together at best. Love, support, cherish, praise, value, and honor each other. Be tender, helpful, sweet, and kind. Respect and court your mate! Make him/her the king/queen of your life. Help the love of your life get to heaven. Never abandon that mission (Col. 3:18–19; Tit. 2:1–5).

6. *Your children.* Don't give up on them. We have but eighteen short years at best to do our job (Deut. 6:4–9). We brought them into this world. Time flies and we must seize the opportunity to turn them to God. Prepare them for eternity. Teach them daily about God.

7. *Others.* Hell is real, so souls are at stake (Matt. 25:31–46). That fact alone should compel us never to give up on a soul. The lost are really lost! Have you been to a funeral lately?

8. *Self* (Matt. 22:29). You can be of great use to God and others. Don't give up!

QUESTIONS

1. The only thing that really matters is to _____ in the Lord.
2. So, never _____ up, don't die on _____ and don't stop too _____ or you will _____ it all.
3. Everything in life and each new _____ are not always "the _____ of the _____."
4. God cannot use a _____ person!
5. God may _____, but He will not _____ His children.
6. Jesus did not establish his church to _____ anyone.
7. _____ is powerful and will _____ things.
8. A great _____ will turn to and _____ God and the _____ (Ps. 33:12).
9. There are _____ at stake and _____ is real (Matt. 25:31-46).
10. You can be of great use to _____ and _____.

TRUE OR FALSE

1. ____ God does not want anyone to give up.
2. ____ Neither the devil nor any person can make you give up.
3. ____ When discouraged, we can turn to the church for solace.
4. ____ Prayer is never mentioned in connection with our Lord's life.
5. ____ We should love this nation and our flag, and should pray for our future.

FIVE SIMPLE QUESTIONS

1. Is it ever right to ask, "Why me, Lord?" Give two examples.
2. Why is it important never to give up on your mate?
3. What kind of morals do we often see in society?
4. What should be a little bit of heaven on earth?
5. Since God is in control, what personal thoughts and emotions of yours is He able to hear and see? (Isa. 38:5).

8

ABOUT ALCOHOL, DRUGS, AND TOBACCO

PURPOSE
To reveal the harm and sin this "three-headed monster" brings upon society.

GOAL
To show that the Bible condemns all three of these.

CHALLENGING THOUGHT
Seven hundred thousand people die yearly as a result of these three evils.

KEY WORDS

sin	harm	influence
habit	gods	death
suffering		

CHOICES BEFORE US
It is either king alcohol, drugs, and tobacco, or King Jesus.

THREE GREAT TRUTHS
Whatever you eat, it should be to the glory of God.
Whatever you drink, it should be to the glory of God.
Whatever you do, it should be to the glory of God.

SCRIPTURES TO BE READ AND STUDIED

1 Corinthians 3:16–17	1 Corinthians 10:31
Psalm 101:3	Habakkuk 2:10
3 John 2	Romans 14:21
1 Thessalonians 5:22	1 Timothy 5:22
Galatians 5:19–21	2 Peter 2:19

PRAYER FOR TODAY

Heavenly Father, help us to abstain from sinful habits.

Introduction

It is shocking how alcohol, drugs, and tobacco are "glorified" even though they bring havoc upon society. Usually, alcohol and other drugs that condemned, but not tobacco, even by Christians. Most preachers avoid even discussing it. This study will take a look at all three. Accept the challenge: honestly examine the evidence presented. First and foremost, all three are sinful. I pray that we can convince our young people of this truth.

Alcohol

A casual reading of the Bible will reveal the sin of drinking alcohol (Hab. 2:15; Gal. 5:19; 1 Cor. 6:10; Prov. 20:1). Noah was guilty (Gen. 9:20–28) and so was Lot (Gen. 19:30–38). Between 125,000 and 150,000 persons die each year because of beer, wine, whiskey, and other alcoholic drinks. Alcohol destroys homes, creates orphans, and degrades society. There is no such thing as "social fornication. Neither is there such thing as a "social drinker." If a person drinks only one beer or one glass of wine, he is one drink drunk. Graveyards are full of "social drinkers."

The bottom line is that imbibing alcoholic beverages is a sin. Jesus did not make fermented wine at the wedding in John 2. I know that because He never sinned.

Drugs

We are facing a sad and horrible drug crisis—marijuana, crack cocaine, heroine, whatever! Most heroine addicts (85 percent) started with marijuana. This year, some 25,000 will die from heroine and cocaine alone. The "and such like" in Galatians 5:19–21 will prove these to be sin. Someone might say, "Well, where in the Bible does it say, 'Thou shalt not use dope'?" The same place it says that sniffing glue, drinking hair oil, smelling cleaning fluid, or baptizing gorillas is wrong! A sinful prohibition does not have to be specifically mentioned. Where does the Bible say, "Thou shalt not pour acid into your baby's eye"? Scriptures like Galatians 5:19–21, along with common sense, answer the question. Robberies, murders, rapes, suicides, and many other societal ills are linked to drug use. Yes, it takes a "dope" to use dope.

It is sad that in today's society, many folks do not go to a boot-legger or liquor store to get a "buzz." They get their highs from prescription drugs. Many are absolutely hooked. They get the same buzz from prescription drugs that they get from whiskey.

Also, myriads of children with so–called attention deficit disorder (ADD) are doped with a legal drug just because parents do not take the time to teach, train, and discipline them. That is a shame in our society. Parents, please consider this.

Tobacco

Now the fur begins to fly! I do not believe smokers are third rate citizens, but I am fully convinced they are sinning. Smokeless tobacco (snuff), cigars, and cigarettes are in this group. If tobacco were newly discovered, its sale to the general public would be illegal. More Columbians die from American cigarettes than Americans die from Columbian dope! Daily deaths resulting from tobacco use are equal to that of two full jumbo jets crashing with no survivors. Wayne McLaren, a "Marlboro man," died of lung cancer. He said, "Anyone with the IQ of a hamster knows better than to use tobacco." He went on to apologize for helping kill people. History verifies that folks knew as early as 1604 that tobacco harmed and killed people! We now have documented proof that the tobacco industry knew in 1953 that tobacco was lethal. Someone has well described it as "a fire on one end and a fool on the other." My own daddy smoked for some sixty years. Besides the money spent, he smoked a Camel approximately sixty miles long. The tobacco industry is the biggest dope dealer in America! This year alone, a half-million people will die from the use of tobacco!

One of the elders where I preached in 1986 was a tobacco farmer. I preached against smoking, chewing, and dipping, and—you guessed it!—I was fired. But thirteen people publicly responded to the Lord's invitation and vowed to quit using tobacco. An R. J. Reynolds executive said, "We don't smoke the _____. We just sell it to the young, poor, black, and the stupid." Now what does that tell you? The cost—besides the deaths—is staggering.

Objections Answered (1 Cor. 10:31; 3 John 2)

1. *What about coffee and tea?* Where is the evidence that they kill and destroy?
2. *I will die one day anyway.* Why bring suffering and death on faster by using tobacco?
3. *People die of cancer who don't smoke.* Not everyone who attempts suicide dies.
4. *It is my life.* True, but this year some fifty thousand will die from second hand smoke.
5. *You do not want me to have any fun.* Yes, I do, the right kind of fun.
6. *It is not wrong.* What about your influence? Does it harm your body? (2 Pet. 2:19).
7. *I just smoke cigars and dip.* Same results: cancer and horrible deaths.
8. *I know preachers who smoke or dip.* Some preachers fornicate, curse, and use dope.
9. *What is wrong with it?* The smell, the cost, your health, and your enslavement.
10. *I like it.* Would you recommend it to your children, to your mother, or to Jesus?

Syllogism
Whatever harms the temple (body) of God is sin
    (1 Cor. 3:16–17).
Tobacco harms the temple (body) of God.
Therefore, the use of tobacco is sin.

QUESTIONS

1. It is either king _____, _____ and _____ or King _____.
2. Whatever you _____, _____ or _____, it should be to the glory of _____.
3. A casual reading of the _____ will revel the sin of drinking _____.
4. This year, some _____ will die from _____ and _____ alone.
5. _____, _____, _____, _____ etc. are all linked to drug use.
6. If _____ was newly discovered today, it would be illegal.
7. More _____ die from American _____ than Americans die from _____ dope.
8. This year alone some _____ people will die from the use of tobacco.
9. 125,000–150,000 people die each year because of _____.
10. The "Marlboro Man" said, "Anyone with the IQ of a _____ knows better than to use _____."

TRUE OR FALSE

1. ____ Drinking one glass of wine makes a person one drink drunk.
2. ____ Since the Bible does not say specifically, "Do not smoke marijuana," then it is right to do so.
3. ____ Second-hand smoke will kill fifty thousand people this year.
4. ____ Jesus made alcoholic wine in John 2 because He wanted people to feel good!
5. ____ History verifies that folks knew tobacco was harmful as early as the 17th century.

FIVE SIMPLE QUESTIONS

1. Approximately how many people die yearly from alcohol, drugs, and tobacco?
2. What might an addict experience from the misuse of prescription drugs?
3. What verse in the New Testament uses the phrase, "and such like"?
4. Is harming the body a sin? List two scriptures to support your answer.
5. Does something have to be specifically mentioned and condemned in the Bible for it to be wrong? Give an example.

9

Plain Bible Talk

ABOUT ATTENDANCE

PURPOSE

To challenge every Christian concerning the importance of attendance.

GOAL

To allow the Bible to determine if forsaking the assembly is sin.

CHALLENGING THOUGHT

It is sin to willfully miss the services of the church.

KEY WORDS

heart	truth	appointment
presence	sin	duty
desire	first	

CHOICES BEFORE US

Either Hebrews 10:25 means what it says or it cannot be understood.

THREE GREAT TRUTHS

An attendance problem is a heart problem.

Your empty pew tells on you.

To absent yourself from the assembly is a vote to close the doors of the building.

SCRIPTURES TO BE READ AND STUDIED

Proverbs 23:7	Matthew 6:33
Mark 4:19	Hebrews 10:25–31

PRAYER FOR TODAY
*Dear God, we thank Thee for allowing us to stand in
Thy presence.*

Introduction

The Christian's attendance in worship should have been decided the day he was baptized. Everyone should realize that he has a set appointment with God. Yes, an attendance problem reflects a heart problem (Prov. 23:7). Why do preachers have to spend so much time trying to convince Christians they should attend? Something is wrong with that picture. Non-attendance is really saying, "I love something more than I love God" (Mark 4:19). This is exactly why many do not attend on Sunday and Wednesday nights. They need to kill those "golden calves." As Christians, we are obligated to attend every service (Heb. 10:25). This verse does not say "just on Sunday morning"! Attendance is proving one's love to God (1 Cor. 4:2).

A Guide That Will Keep You Faithful

1. *You are missed when you are absent* (1 Sam. 20:8). Christians miss you, care about you, and pray for you when you are absent. Why were you absent last week? Company come? Too tired? Won't hear or see anything new at church? Children not interested? No one visited you? What was the real excuse for your absence? God is truly grieved when you miss the services. God has a description for you— a clean sow that runs to the mud hole, and a recovering dog that eats again that which made him sick! (2 Pet. 2:20–22). Not a pretty picture, is it? There is no clearer sign that one is losing his love and interest in the blood-bought church than non-attendance. We sincerely miss you, your family, your fellowship, your face, and yes, your contribution. What are you doing with your contribution? We do love and miss you because you are a part of us.

2. *Revive the vow (promise) you made when you were baptized* (Acts 8:37; Heb. 10:23). Prove to God that you still love Him! When we gather to worship, we are approaching God's throne. Are you now saying that you no longer love God or Christ (John 14:15). You are if

you forsake the assembly! Yes, you are telling Jesus He was foolish to die on the cross. It is that serious! Attendance confirms your love and vow.

3. *Don't blame others for not attending.* If you do so, you sin against your own soul (Hab. 2:10). No one and nothing should keep you from worshiping God.

4. *You are a member of the church and a vital part of it.* God expects you to attend (1 Cor. 4:2). In forsaking the assembly, you are saying you do not want to fellowship your spiritual family, study the Bible, or partake of the Lord's supper. You are also saying Jesus died in vain.

5. *Your place will be empty* (1 Sam. 20:25). This includes your encouragement and talents. Just think. You miss the opportunity of being with the Son of God (Matt. 18:20). Christians love you more than anybody on earth! Do you not appreciate and need that?

6. *You affirm that you no longer love Christ* (John 14:15; 21:15–17). If someone were to ask, "Do you love Christ?" would that offend you? You cannot make the claim that you love Him and not attend His assemblies! How can you love Him when you refuse to remember Him in the Lord's supper? Proof is in action, not words.

7. *Non-attendance is a fruit of a heart going bad.* Are you now more faithful, dedicated, knowledgeable, prayerful, and committed? Are you more content? Trusting God more? Happier? Reading the Bible more? More involved in the work of the church? What is happening to your spiritual life and your soul? Read 1 Corinthians 10:12.

8. *Non-attendance is eternally harmful to your family.* Can your children trust you with their hearts? (Prov. 23:26). When you are absent, you are sending your family a strong message that the church is just not that important (Matt. 6:33). On the other hand, when your family and neighbors see your car in the church parking lot, it speaks volumes for your love for Christ. Please get your priorities right. Parents cannot act like the devil six days a week and then be "saints" on Sunday. If you choose to miss Sunday morning and then take the Lord's supper that night, you drink damnation to your soul (1 Cor. 11:29).

9. *You miss the wonderful opportunity to worship God.* As the distance from God increases, so does the size of the crowd. Make no mistake about it. Unfaithfulness in attendance will cost you your soul. You will lose your influence with your friends and neighbors. The church loses a member. God loses a faithful child. Note Hebrews 10:25–31.

- Verse 25: God says not to forsake the assembly—none of them, not just Sunday morning.
- Verse 26: To forsake any assembly is willful sin.
- Verse 27: The cost for willful sin is enormous.
- Verses 28–29: Our plight will be worse than the plight of those under the law of Moses.
- Verses 28–29: When the Christian forsakes the assembly, he has treated Jesus like an old door mat, treated His blood as that of some animal, and looks at the Bible as just another book.
- Verses 30–31: Those guilty of forsaking the assembly will face the wrath of God.

Now, how serious do you take this?

10. *If you are guilty, a public confession is necessary.* Unless our commitment to Christ increases, forsaking the assembly next week will be easier than it was this week! God has done all He can or will do in providing the opportunity for us to worship Him. Why would we not want to attend every service, meet around the Lord's table, be with the saints, proclaim the greatness and goodness of God, affirm the resurrection of Christ, express love and gratitude, and humble ourselves in the very presence of Jehovah God? Why? What more could God have done? He could not have loved us more or provided a better church. Keep Hebrews 10:25 in your heart and know that willfully forsaking the assembly is a sin that will cost you your soul.

QUESTIONS

1. Either Hebrews 10:25 means what it _____ else it cannot be _____.

2. Non-attendance is really saying, "I_____ something more than _____" (Mark 4:19).

3. The _____ attendance was decided the _____ he was _____.
4. When we gather to _____, we are approaching _____ throne.
5. By forsaking, you are saying that you do not want to _____
   your spiritual _____, study the _____, partake of the _____
   _____ , and that _____ died in vain.
6. Non-attendance is a fruit of a _____ going _____.
7. If you choose to miss Sunday _____ and then take the _____
   _____ that night, you drink _____ to your soul (1 Cor. 11:29).
8. According to Hebrews 10:25–31, the Christian that forsakes the
   assembly has treated _____ like an old doormat, treated His
   _____ as that of some animal, and looks at the _____
   as just another book.
9. You affirm that you no longer _____ Christ when you are absent
   (John 14:15; 21:15–17)
10. Christians are _____ to attend _____ service (Heb. 10:25).

TRUE OR FALSE

1. ____ An attendance problem is a heart problem.
2. ____ Hebrews 10:25 says to attend only on Sunday mornings if you
   want to.
3. ____ According to 2 Peter 2:20–22, when a Christian turns back to
   the world, he is as a dog returning to his own vomit.
4. ____ To willfully absent one's self from the assembly is a vote to
   close the doors of the building where the saints are meeting.
5. ____ Faithful attendance is only for radical and fanatical Christians.

FIVE SIMPLE QUESTIONS

1. What scripture teaches that one must seek the kingdom (church)
   first?
2. What verse teaches that it is a fearful thing to fall into the hands of
   the living God?
3. What verse teaches that one can drink damnation to his soul, by
   partaking of the Lord's supper unworthily?
4. What two verses teach the importance of keeping and reviving our
   vow (promise)?
5. What verse teaches that whatever is in the heart is reflected in action?

10

Plain Bible Talk

ABOUT "APPLE OF EDEN" DOCTRINE

PURPOSE
To see how eternally dangerous it is to "think" that the Bible teaches something.

GOAL
To present examples of so-called "apple of Eden" doctrine.

CHALLENGING THOUGHT
Man's think-so does not equal God's said-so!

KEY WORDS

apple	fruit	know
rule	thought	Bible
commands		

CHOICES BEFORE US
Either a person believes what God has said or he will make his own rules.

THREE GREAT TRUTHS
The Bible does not identify the fruit Adam and Eve ate as an apple.

The "apple of Eden" doctrine is still taught today.

Unconcern for God's truth and ignorance of His Word will populate hell.

SCRIPTURES TO BE READ AND STUDIED
Genesis 3:1–5   John 18:34
1 Peter 4:11   Philippians 3:16

PRAYER FOR TODAY
Our Father, give us the wisdom and courage to accept Thy truths.

Introduction

If you were to ask the person on the street what kind of fruit Adam and Eve ate in the garden, he would reply, "An apple." Many jokes, poems, and songs have been written about the apple of Eden. Even members of the church often say it was an apple, even though a lady once told me it was a pear. All this confirms the sad truth that most people believe something is taught in the Bible when in reality it is not. Question: Where in the Bible does it say this fruit was an apple? It is not to be found! It is truly sad in view of eternity that so many are misguided to this extent (John 18:34). Thus, our lesson: "Apple-of-Eden Doctrine."

Examples of "Apple of Eden" Religion

1. *Three wise men visited Christ in Matthew 2.* The Bible says wise men but does not specify their number.

2. *Near the end of time, we will not be able to tell one season from another.* Yes we will (Gen. 8:22).

3. *The Lord shaved with a razor* (Isa. 7:20). The razor God used was the king of Assyria. The king shaved (punished) the Jews.

4. *John spoke of the Catholic church in the book of Revelation.* Where is the scripture reference?

5. *Elijah went to heaven in a chariot of fire.* No, it was by a whirlwind (2 Kings 2:11).

6. *Paul wrote fourteen New Testament books, including Hebrews.* Paul said he signed every epistle that he wrote (2 Thess. 3:17), and he did not sign Hebrews.

7. *There are twelve "minor" prophets and five "major" prophets.* Where is such ever stated or hinted at in the Bible? What is "minor" about

Joel or Hosea? Are there "minor" apostles? Epistles? Let's now study other "apple of Eden" doctrines that are taught every day.

Ten Examples

When people think what they have been taught is right without checking the Bible, souls are lost! "Behold, I thought" will carry many to torment. Saul of Tarsus thought he was right; he was wrong (Acts 26:9). So was Uzzah (2 Sam. 6:1–7). A man patted a strange dog on the head thinking it was friendly; it wasn't! A man struck a match to see if his gas tank was empty; it wasn't! A man thought he could beat the train barreling down the track; he didn't! Man thinks the fruit in Genesis 3 was an apple; the Bible does not tell us that!

Note the following examples of "apple of Eden" doctrine.

1. *There is a difference in the moral and ceremonial law of Moses.* The Bible says the tables of stone, the covenant, and the law were all the same thing, and were nailed to the cross (1 Kings 8:9, 21; Deut. 10:1–4; Col. 2:14). The whole law, not just part of it, was taken out of the way.

2. *Peter was the first pope of the Catholic church.* The Bible does not teach this. Peter had a mother-in-law, so he was married. There is no proof that he was ever in Rome. Besides this, the Catholic church was not established until AD 325 and Peter had been dead some 250 years. Read Matthew 8:14 and 1 Corinthians 9:5.

3. *Addressing preachers as Reverend, Pastor, or Father is appropriate.* The masses have been taught to give respect to "men of the cloth" in this fashion, and they do so without checking the scriptures. Read Matthew 23:1–12 and 1 Timothy 3:1–7. God should be exalted above all men (Ps. 111:9). It is a sin to elevate man in such a manner. Yea, it is blasphemy!

4. *Faith only will save.* The very opposite is stated so plainly that anyone can understand it (James 2:24). "Add to your faith . . ." (2 Pet. 1:5). "Believe and be baptized" (Mark 16:16). What part of James 2:24 do folks not understand?

5. *One church is as good as another.* If one is speaking of denominational churches, he is right. But that does not apply to the blood-

bought church, the church of Christ (Matt. 16:18; Acts 20:28; Eph. 1:22–23; 4:4–6; Rom. 16:16). Is one God or Lord as good as another? Folks who make this statement are practicing true "apple of Eden" religion.

6. *Using instrumental music in worship is acceptable.* To man, but not to God! Read Ephesians 5:19; 2 Peter 1:3; Acts 20:20. Instruments were introduced in "Christian" worship in the seventh century. No one can defend the instrument in worship and stay in the New Testament one second!

7. *One is saved before baptism.* Again, "apple of Eden" religion rears its unscriptural head! First Peter 3:21; Acts 2:38; and Acts 22:16 do away with this foolish doctrine. It is not Bible.

8. *Names do not matter.* I beg to differ (Acts 4:12; 11:26; Phil. 2:10; 1 Pet. 4:16). They matter to God–and to you! Did you name your child Spot, Jezebel, or Ding Dong Head? Why not?

9. *Salvation can be found outside the church.* If so, Christ died for naught (Acts 20:28). This is a very dangerous way of saying that the fruit in Genesis 3 was an apple. This is found in man's imagination (Acts 2:38, 47; Eph.1:3; 3:21; 5:23; Gal. 3:26–27; 2 Tim. 2:10).

10. *My preacher said . . .* Now we come to the source of "apple of Eden" religion (Matt. 15:8–14; Gal. 1:8–9; 4:30; 1 Pet. 4:11). None of the "apple of Eden" doctrines are from God but from man! Always demand a "thus saith the Lord" in spiritual matters.

QUESTIONS

1. Either one _____ what God has said or he will make his own _____.

2. The Bible does not say that the _____ Adam and Eve ate was an _____.

3. The whole _____ was taken out of the _____, not just _____ of it.

4. It is a sin to elevate man in such a manner (calling him Father or Reverend), yea it is _____.

5. Is one _____ or Lord as good as another?
6. No one can defend the _____ in worship and stay in the New Testament one _____.
7. Always demand a "_____ _____ ___ _____" in all matters.
8. If you were to ask the average person on the _____ what kind of _____ did Adam and Eve eat in the _____, they would reply, "___ _____."
9. An example of "Apple of Eden" religion is to teach that _____ wise _____ visited Christ in Matthew 2.
10. Whenever people "think" what they have been _____ is right without checking the _____, souls are _____!

TRUE OR FALSE

1. ____ Elijah went to heaven in a chariot of fire.
2. ____ The razor the Lord used for shaving (Isa. 7:20) was not a literal razor.
3. ____ According to 2 Thessalonians 3:17, Paul signed every epistle he wrote.
4. ____ The Bible calls some of the books of the prophets "Minor Prophets."
5. ____ One can know the identity of the fruit Adam and Eve ate.

FIVE SIMPLE QUESTIONS

1. What Bible verse calls the fruit Adam and Eve ate an apple?
2. What verse teaches the seasons will always be as we now know them?
3. What verse says that no one is saved by faith only?
4. Are "apple of Eden" doctrines from God or man?
5. Compare man's think-so to God's said-so.

11

Plain Bible Talk

ABOUT THE LORD'S SUPPER

PURPOSE
To know why Christians partake of the Lord's supper every week.

GOAL
To determine why the church of Christ observes the Lord's supper every Sunday.

CHALLENGING THOUGHT
When a Christian partakes of the Lord's supper unworthily, he drinks damnation to his soul (1 Cor. 11:29).

KEY WORDS

Sunday	every	fruit of the vine
blood	body	unleavened bread
cross		

CHOICES BEFORE US
Either the Lord's supper is sacred worship or it is a common meal.

THREE GREAT TRUTHS
The Lord's supper represents the body and blood of the Lord.
It is the greatest memorial known to man.
Only a Christian is to partake of it.

SCRIPTURES TO BE READ AND STUDIED
Matthew 26:26–28   1 Corinthians 11: 20–34
Acts 20:7

PRAYER FOR TODAY
Dear God, we thank Thee for the blood-stained cross.

1. *Jesus instituted the Lord's supper on the night in which He was betrayed* (Matt. 26:26–30). To prepare for the Passover, He sent Peter and John into Jerusalem to meet a man carrying a pitcher of water. He would show them a large upper room, furnished and prepared. There they were to arrange a meeting place (Luke 22:1–22). There would be a lamb without blemish, unleavened bread, bitter herbs, and fruit of the vine. Jesus chose from these four items the two for the Lord's supper that would represent His body and blood. No other items can ever be used with God's approval! This supper is called the "breaking of bread" (Acts 2:42; 20:7), "communion" (1 Cor. 10:16–17), "Lord's supper" (1 Cor. 11:20) and the "Lord's table" (1 Cor. 10:21). Never is it called the "Eucharist" or a "sacrament."

2. *Who is qualified to partake of it?* The answer: Christians (Matt. 26:26–28; Acts 2:38–47; 20:7; 1 Cor. 11:20–34). It is to be eaten (observed) in the kingdom—the church (Matt. 16:16–19; 26:26–29). Only those in the church are qualified and privileged to partake! The non-Christian must qualify himself by obeying the gospel and therefore becoming a member of the church of Christ in order to partake. Jesus wants to commune with everybody but will do so only with the children of His house (1 Tim. 3:15).

3. *Christians are to partake every Sunday.* Why? Because the Bible says so (Acts 20:7; 1 Cor. 11:20). If we never knew another reason, that one is enough. Also note 1 Corinthians 16:1–2. There is a first day in every week—Sunday. Did the Jews have to ask if Exodus 20:8 meant every Sabbath? No! To partake of the Lord's supper on a day other than Sunday is sin (Rev. 22:18–19). Some have argued that if Acts 20:7 were not in the Bible, then we could not prove that we are

to partake every Sunday. This is foolishness gone to seed because Acts 20:7 *is* in the Bible! When one understands the purpose of the Lord's supper and the frequency it is to be eaten, he will then stop trying to argue it away.

4. *Partaking of the Lord's supper is at the very heart of the Christian's worship.* Redemption is the Bible's singular theme and the Lord's supper is the summation of redemption. The partaking must be done in the way, time, and manner that God has prescribed. Every Christian must appreciate the exalted honor and privilege of communing with the Master when partaking of the Lord's supper. It must be eaten in a thoughtful manner (1 Cor. 11:27–30). I am convinced that a failure to recognize this privilege is one of the major reasons, if not *the* major reason, many are unfaithful in their attendance. Why would anyone choose not to commune with and remember Jesus?

5. *In partaking, we remember Jesus' death till He comes again* (1 Cor. 11:24–26). Our every thought must be directed upon the very purpose of it. We also remember the blood-stained cross while partaking. It is a time of self-examination, a time to discern—to judge thoroughly, to recognize—the Lord's body. It is a time of fellowship with Christ. It serves as a time for each Christian to survey the events of Calvary and to remember these things: one Lord, two thieves, three crosses, four parts of His garment, five wounds, six agonizing hours on the cross, and seven precious sayings He uttered.

6. *Never is the term* wine *used in connection with the Lord's supper.* Unfermented fruit of the vine (juice) was used. Nowhere, inside or outside the Bible, do we have any authority to use fermented wine. What better represents the Lord's blood, fermented or unfermented? It was always unleavened bread and fruit of the vine (Luke 22:1–23). We now have proof that they had ways to preserve unfermented juice all year.

7. *There is no biblical authority to sing while we partake of the Lord's supper.* Why would anyone want to participate in two acts of worship at the same time? These two acts of worship involve different

physical, mental, and spiritual participation. Each demands our total concentration. It would be just as appropriate to sing while someone leads in prayer (1 Cor. 14:40). Why can everyone not give each act of worship full and undivided attention? Worship is something we do, not something done to us. It demands our full attention. Note that Jesus and His disciples ate and then sang a hymn! (Matt. 26:26–30).

8. *How many cups must we use?* In Luke 22:17 *cup* refers to the contents. Using one container is certainly acceptable, but it is not binding. Jacob dug a well, but the emphasis was always on the water, not the hole! (John 4:12). If an assembly of the saints cannot use but one container, how large was the container used in the Jerusalem church? (Acts 2:41; 4:4). Eighteen and one-half gallons! It would have taken more than twenty hours for all to partake! Using many containers is sanitary, convenient, and biblical. After all, Jesus told the disciples to divide the contents among themselves.

QUESTIONS

1. When a _____ fails to properly partake of the _____ _____, he drinks _____ to his soul (1 Cor. 11:29).
2. _____ instituted the Lord's supper on the night in which He was _____ (Matt. 26:26–30).
3. _____ are to partake every _____.
4. To partake of the Lord's supper on a _____ other than Sunday is _____.
5. In partaking, we _____ Jesus' _____ till He comes again.
6. Never is the term _____ used in connection with the Lord's supper.
7. _____ demands our full _____ and is something we do, not something done unto us.
8. The word "cup" refers to the _____.
9. In partaking of the Lord's supper, one would do well to remember: _____ Lord, _____ thieves, _____ crosses, _____ parts of his

garment, _____ wounds, _____ agonizing hours on the cross and those _____ precious sayings He uttered.

10. Never does the Bible call the Lord's Supper the "_____" or "_____."

True or False

1. ____ The Bible also calls the Lord's supper the "breaking of bread."
2. ____ Exodus 20:8 did not mean every Sabbath.
3. ____ The Bible authorizes us to partake the Lord's supper on the day of our choice.
4. ____ There is no Bible authority to sing while partaking of the Lord's supper.
5. ____ Only Christians are qualified to partake of the Lord's supper.

Five Simple Questions

1. What does the Bible teach about the number of containers congregations should use to serve the cup, the fruit of the vine?
2. What four different items made up the Passover feast?
3. What two disciples (apostles) did Jesus send to arrange for a place to observe the Passover feast?
4. Of what benefit is partaking of the unleavened bread and fruit of the vine to a non-Christian?
5. What is the greatest memorial known to man?

12

Plain Bible Talk

ABOUT ANSWERING OUR FAMILIES AND FRIENDS

PURPOSE
To present examples on how to answer questions from our families and friends.

GOAL
To learn better how to teach our families and friends.

CHALLENGING THOUGHT
The purpose of asking and answering questions is to learn truth.

KEY WORDS

why	how	when
where	responsible	knowledge
lost	salvation	

CHOICES BEFORE US
Either we will teach others truth or they will continue to believe lies.

THREE GREAT TRUTHS
A person cannot teach what he does not know.
The lost are really lost.
Christians are responsible to teach others the truth.

SCRIPTURES TO BE READ AND STUDIED
2 Timothy 2:2   1 Peter 3:15
John 6:45   Ezekiel 3:16–21

PRAYER FOR TODAY
Dear God, give us the wisdom and courage to tell others the truth.

Introduction

We must never forget the value of a soul and that the lost are really lost! In our materialistic society, we do not "find" the time to teach others. Family and friends are sometimes the hardest to teach, but there is no better place to start (Mark 5:19). God says that we shine as the stars of heaven when we make the effort to teach others (Dan. 12:2–3). Always remember that you are speaking for God, and those who say sarcastic things about you are really attacking Him. It can be disappointing, but we must make the effort. The time will come when your family and friends will question you concerning your conversion and the church of Christ. There will be things they simply do not understand, things with which they disagree. A scriptural answer must be given at all times. Yes, there will be times when questions are asked to trap you or to draw you into an argument, but always give the questioner the benefit of the doubt and be ready to answer (1 Pet. 3:15). Hint: Always encourage students to read the answers from the Bible for themselves! The seed must be planted. The following are examples of some often asked questions from our families and friends:

1. *Do you really believe that we can see the Bible alike?*
   What does the Bible say? It says we can, so for us to say otherwise is to accuse God of not being capable of making the Bible understandable. The Bible is the standard of judgment (John 12:48), it was written to be understood (Eph. 3:3–4), and it has all the right answers (Ps. 119:128). Examples: Who was the first man? Who was Jesus' mother? Who built the ark? See, we can understand it alike.

2. *Why does the church of Christ not believe in music?*
   What does the Bible say? Yes, we do believe in music—the kind au-

thorized by God (Eph. 5:18–19). We sing with our voices and from our hearts. We do not add to that, just as we do not add gravy and biscuits to the Lord's supper. We do not add the instrument for the same reason we do not meow like cats while we worship in song. We believe we should do all things in the way God said to do them. Thus, we do exactly what God said to do; we sing and do not make sounds with instrumental music. There is no biblical authority for the instrument.

3. *If baptism is necessary for salvation, then what about the thief on the cross?*

What does the Bible say? There is no *if* about it; the Bible says baptism is necessary (Acts 2:38; 22:16; Mark 16:16; 1 Pet. 3:21; Gal. 3:26–27). That settles the matter. The thief lived and died while the Old Testament was still valid (Col. 2:14; Heb. 7:22; 8:6–7; 9:16–17). When Jesus taught him, all Jews were subject to Moses' law. The great commission had not been given, so the thief died before baptism was necessary for salvation. Here is an illustration: Abraham Lincoln never paid income tax. He lived and died before the IRS was formed, therefore he was not liable to pay income taxes. Neither was the thief "liable" to be baptized for the remission of sins.

4. *What if a person has believed and repented, but dies before he is baptized. Are you saying he is lost?*

What does the Bible say? Yes, although I have never heard of this happening. Your question is the same as asking if a man is saved if he dies before he believes. A person cannot be saved if he has not fulfilled the obedience required by God. This obedience involves baptism (Acts 2:38, 47). No one is a part of the church—the bride of Christ (2 Cor. 11:2; Rev. 21:2, 9–10)—apart from baptism. Being baptized allows us to be a part of Jesus' bride. Question: If a man is on his way to the church building to be married and meets with a fatal accident, is he married to the woman waiting on him? Why not?

5. *Do you believe that members of the church of Christ are the only ones going to heaven?*

What does the Bible say? No. Babies and those born mentally handicapped will be in heaven. Answer: Yes, an accountable person must be a member of the one blood-bought church to be saved. If not, then God lied to us! Please read the following scriptures: Matthew 16:18; Acts 2:38, 47; 20:28; Romans 16:16; Ephesians 1:22–23; 4:4; 5:23. The unfaithful members of the church of Christ will not make it (Rev. 2:10). Only a few, in comparison to all who shall live, will make it (Matt. 7:21). We want you to be in heaven.

6. *If the church of Christ is right, then are you saying my mother is lost in hell?*

What does the Bible say? Yes, if she died outside Christ (2 Tim. 2:10). I am no one's judge, but the Bible answers your question (John 12:48). What your mother believed or did not believe has no bearing on your eternal salvation. Even if your mother is lost, her judgment is set and cannot be changed. You will stand before God as an individual (Rom. 14:12; 2 Cor. 5:10), and there are no changes after death. What purpose would it serve if you and your loved ones are in hell together? If you go to heaven and your mother goes to hell, you will not have that knowledge and memory (Eccles. 9:5, 10). Obey and teach your family while there is time. Hell is not worth it and heaven is worth it all.

7. *Are you saying one church is not as good as another?*

What does the Bible say? Yes. There is only one blood-bought church (Acts 20:28). All others will be rooted up (Matt. 15:13). One man-made church is as good as the next. Jesus will save only those in His church (Eph. 5:23). Is one medicine as good as another? Doctor? Name? No one was ever added to a denomination in the first century; denominations did not exist.

QUESTIONS

1. One cannot _____ what he does not know.
2. We must never forget the _____ of a soul and that the _____ are really _____.
3. God says we are "_____" when we make the effort to _____ others (Dan 12:2–3).
4. The time will come when your _____ and _____ will question you concerning your _____ and the _____ of Christ.
5. A _____ answer must be given at all _____.
6. The Bible is the _____ of judgment (John 12:48); it was written to be _____ (Eph. 3:3–4) and it has all the right _____ (Ps. 119:128).
7. No one is a part of the _____ (the bride of Christ, 2 Cor. 11:2; Rev. 21:2, 9, 10) apart from _____.
8. Yes, accountable _____ must be a member of the _____ _____ church to be saved.
9. _____ is not worth it and _____ is worth it all.
10. One _____ church is as good as the _____.

TRUE OR FALSE

1. ____ As Christians, we are responsible to teach others the truth.
2. ____ We can understand the Bible alike.
3. ____ There are many scriptures to prove that instrumental music in worship is scriptural.
4. ____ One can change his dead mother's eternal destiny.
5. ____ No one was ever added to a denomination in the first century.

FIVE SIMPLE QUESTIONS

1. What is the purpose of asking and answering questions?
2. What are some wrong motives for asking Bible questions?
3. What act of obedience makes us a part of the bride of Christ?
4. What changes will we be able to make after death?
5. What scriptures teach that we will have no knowledge or memory of our lost loved ones?

13

Plain Bible Talk

ABOUT RIGHT AND WRONG

Purpose
To learn how to tell right from wrong and the consequences of each.

Goal
To determine from the Bible what are the right and the wrong things to do.

Challenging Thought
The only way to know what is right and wrong is to know what the one and only right standard, the Bible, says on any given subject.

Key Words
sin	right	wrong
feelings	conscience	common sense

Choices Before Us
Any thought, action, or intent is either right or wrong.

Three Great Truths
There is no right way to do a wrong thing.
When a person is finished with sin, sin is not finished with him.
Wrong is always wrong.

SCRIPTURES TO BE READ AND STUDIED
1 Corinthians 4:9   Titus 2:7–8
Isaiah 5:20; 55:8–9   Proverbs 16:25
3 John 11

PRAYER FOR TODAY
Dear God, help us to know right from wrong and then to do the right.

Wrong Standards in Determining Right from Wrong
- Feelings (Prov. 16:25)
- Conscience (Acts 23:1)
- Visions (Gal. 1:6–9)
- Personal opinions (Jer. 10:23)
- Human creeds (Matt. 15:8–9)

The Right Standard in Determining Right from Wrong: The Bible!
(2 Tim. 3:16–17; Ps. 119:128; 2 Cor. 5:10; John 12:48)

Unsafe Methods in Deciding Right from Wrong
1. *Everyone else is doing it.* What if everyone else were drinking kerosene? Read Exodus 23:2.
2. *I like it.* Many like dope, pornography, and gambling. Read 1 John 2:15–17.
3. *It does not hurt anyone.* Neither does cussing with every breath in the shower, but it hurts self, and God hears and sees all. Read Romans 2:16; 14:7.
4. *I can afford it.* That being the case, then all rich folks will be saved. Read Zephaniah 1:18.
5. *I have done this a long time and nothing bad has happened.* Noah was six hundred years old when the flood came. Time does not alter God's law. Read Psalm 119:89.
6. *My conscience does not bother me.* So it is with the thief, murderer, and homosexual. Read 1 Corinthians 6:9–11.

Every Wrong Thing Is Not Specifically Listed in the Bible

The Bible does not provide a complete list of "do's" and "don'ts." Example: The Bible nowhere says it is wrong to pour acid into a baby's eye, but we all know it is. We are told how to treat people. Furthermore, we are told to treat others as we want to be treated.

- Some things are always wrong (Gal. 5:19–21).
- Some things are always right (Gal. 5:22–23).
- Some things are wrong by the use of them: speech, abuse when disciplining a child, overeating, drinking water in public from a whiskey bottle.
- Some things ordinarily right become wrong under certain circumstances: marriage, sex, and becoming an elder, for example.

Some Questions That Should Help in Your Determination

- Is it allowed or condemned in the Bible?
- Is there any doubt or question in my mind about it?
- Will my doing this cause others to stumble?
- Will this hurt my body or my health?
- Will I develop wrong desires or be tempted in a way that would hinder my Christianity?
- Will it harm or hurt my influence with others?
- Will doing this cause me to compromise my service to God?
- Would Jesus do this?
- If I do this thing, will Jesus be glorified and honored?
- Will it make me stronger and magnify my image for Christ?
- Will this harm the church here?

Things to Consider

1. *Always use good common sense*—horse sense, the old folk called it. This will discourage you from playing Russian roulette, sniffing glue, picking up snakes, or seeing how fast a car will go.
2. *Practice the Golden Rule.* That will discourage cheating, not playing by the rules, bribing others, practicing deception, and telling "white" lies or half truths.

3. *Think about your character, honesty, dignity, and reputation* when it comes to the type of speech, entertainment, music, and "fun" you choose. Always strive to better yourself.

4. *Consider the publicity of your choices.* Would you really want your habits, thoughts, or actions to be known? Would you bathe in public? Why display your bad choices?

5. *Give thought concerning your friends.* Would you want your best friend to find this out? Always consider there is a closer Friend who is watching—Jesus!

6. *Think about your parents, mate, or children.* Would doing this honor them?

7. *Before you do anything, take a look into the future.* Will you have to say, "I never thought it would come to this." Always take the safe course in all you do. Your influence is like your shadow, it follows you everywhere!

QUESTIONS

1. Any _____, action, or _____ is either right, or it is
   _____.
2. Five wrong standards to determine right from wrong are _____
   (Prov. 16:25), _____ (Acts 23:1), _____ (Gal. 1:6–9),
   _____ _____ (Jer. 10:23) and _____
   _____ (Matt. 15:8–9).
3. The one standard is the _____ (John 12:48).
4. Every wrong thing is not specifically listed in the _____.
5. Some things are ordinarily right but sometime becomes _____
   for certain _____.
6. One should ask himself, "Would doing this _____ the church?"
7. Always use good old _____ sense.
8. Before you do anything, take a look into the "_____."
9. There is no _____ way to do a _____ thing.
10. Some things are always _____ (Gal. 5:19–21).

TRUE OR FALSE

1. ____ When one is finished with sin, there are no consequences that
   follow.
2. ____ Since the Bible does not specifically mention and condemn pour-
   ing acid into a baby's eye, it is therefore not wrong.
3. ____ Some things are always right.
4. ____ Some things are wrong by the use of them.
5. ____ A good method to follow is to say that everyone is doing it.

FIVE SIMPLE QUESTIONS

1. When is it right for a Christian to do wrong?
2. How much time must elapse before a wrong deed that has been
   committed becomes right?
3. Why is character, honesty, and dignity important when trying to
   determine a course of action?
4. Since your influence follows you like a shadow, what course of action
   should you always take?
5. What did David think of God's precepts (laws)?

14

Plain Bible Talk

ABOUT THE BLOOD-STAINED CROSS

PURPOSE
To see the preciousness and the seriousness concerning the events at Calvary.

GOAL
To allow these events to permeate our daily walk with the Master.

CHALLENGING THOUGHT
The cross is the culmination of God's love for us.

KEY WORDS

cross	blood	forgiveness
sin	love	crucifixion
agony	scourge	death

CHOICES BEFORE US
Either the events at Calvary really happened or the Bible is a fake.

THREE GREAT TRUTHS
Nothing is more precious than the blood of Christ.
Thanks be unto God for His unspeakable gift.
If not for Calvary, hell would be our eternal home.

SCRIPTURES TO BE READ AND STUDIED

Matthew 26:26–29	Acts 20:7
2 Timothy 2:8	1 Corinthians 11:20–34
Matthew 26–28	1 Corinthians 15:1–4
Mark 14–16	Luke 22–24
John 19–21	

PRAYER FOR TODAY

Our heavenly Father, with all our being, we thank Thee for Calvary.

Introduction

First of all, the author of this material realizes that he cannot do justice to this subject! There are some 333 prophecies of Christ found in the Old Testament and each one came to pass (e.g., Acts 13:29). The birth, death, and resurrection were all prophesied (Gen. 3, Isa. 53, Ps. 16). From the time God announced the birth of Christ until He came into the world (Gen 3:15; Matt. 1:21), 3,960 years went by. The cross confirms the validity of all sixty-six books of the Bible! Calvary was the event the world had been longing for. Yes, I believe in the one they call Jesus! Without Calvary and the resurrection, His birth would mean nothing. The blood-stained cross is the central theme of all the Bible.

Jesus, Our Greatest Friend!

Jesus is our ever-constant companion; He gives purpose and plan to our lives; He has prepared our eternal home; He has forgiven our sins, if we have obeyed the gospel; and He has given us peace of mind. The Lord's supper, made possible by Calvary, is the greatest memorial known to man, and it represents the great and precious events at Calvary. The pale piece of bread and the fruit of the vine are the greatest of all memorials! Those emblems have no equal. Why would any Christian willfully miss partaking of them? No movie has captured—nor will one ever—the seriousness of the events around the cross! Without doubt, it is the greatest story ever told. Jesus should be the ever-present guest in our homes. "Oh, How I Love Jesus" should be our daily song and practice.

His Arrest, Trial, and Crucifixion

Jesus was arrested shortly before midnight. By daylight He had been tried, convicted, and sentenced to suffer on the cross. The entire trial was a joke! Jesus had stood before Annas, Caiaphas, Pilate, Herod, and back to Pilate by 6:00 AM. He had been slapped, spat upon, beaten, mocked, struck, taunted, blindfolded, and scourged. The accusers had fun with Jesus. They put a robe on Him, gave Him a stick for a staff, placed a crown of thorns upon His head, and made sport of Him. One struck the crown and drove its thorns into His skull. The scourging was an awful thing! A whip called the scorpion was used. It had nine leather strips, and each strip had pieces of either glass, bone, or lead tied to their ends. By daylight Jesus was a bloody mess. His back looked like a package of fresh ground hamburger meat! He was virtually unrecognizable.

Before leaving Pilate's hall, they ripped the robe off His back, causing more bleeding. They then placed on his back a cross weighing a little more than a hundred pounds and six feet in length. Calvary was about one-third of a mile away. The executioner compelled Simon to carry it.

Reaching Calvary, they ripped His clothes off, except for His under clothes, and placed Jesus on the cross. Soldiers then nailed five-inch spikes through His wrists and feet. They placed (dropped) the cross into the hole. He was there for six terrible and agonizing hours. The insects, shame, taunting, cramps, blood pressure, racing heartbeat, nerves like violin strings, and the fact that He had to push up to breathe but could not exhale was a death unimaginable!

When the death had to be hastened, soldiers broke their victims' legs with a four-foot board, three inches wide and one inch thick. Jesus died before that terrible act had to be performed. God's only begotten Son died a horrible death for you and me. He endured intense suffering in order to purchase the church! (Acts 20:28).

Around the Cross

Who was there, witnessing the suffering of our Lord?

- The scribes, Pharisees, priests, and Levites who represented powerful Jewish sects.
- The blood-thirsty mob who followed blind leadership.
- The sacrilegious soldiers who carried out the crucifixion.

- The centurion who confessed the Lord but offered no further encouragement.
- The one who ran to give Jesus a drink.
- Simon, who carried the cross for our Savior.
- Two thieves, one who feared God and one who did not.
- Peter, who had denied the Lord.
- The disciples who had forsaken Him.
- The godly women who always stood near Him.
- His mother who never would have abandoned Him.

Question: Which group are you in?

What Jesus Said While on the Cross

Jesus uttered seven precious sayings while on the cross:

1. "Father, forgive them for they know not what they do."
2. "Today thou shalt be with me in paradise."
3. "Behold, thy mother."
4. "I thirst."
5. "My God, my God, why hast thou forsaken me?"
6. "It is finished."
7. "Into thy hands I commend my spirit."

Because of His deep love for us, the Son of God willingly gave His life!

Decision Time

Are you crucifying Jesus again? (Heb. 6:6). Do you love Him? (John 14:15). Brothers and sisters, please read Hebrews 10:25–31; Mark 4:19; and Matthew 6:33.

Non-Christians friends, please read Acts 2:38–47; 20:28; Ephesians 1:22–23, 4:4; and 5:23. In view of Calvary, how dare anyone deny and reject these scriptures! Now, what say ye?

Questions

1. The _____ is the culmination of God's _____ for us.
2. Nothing is more precious than the _____ of Christ.
3. The _____ confirms the validity of all _____ books of the _____.
4. The _____ _____ (made possible by Calvary) is the greatest memorial known to _____ and it represents the great and _____ events at _____.
5. Without _____ and the _____, His birth would mean nothing.
6. Jesus was arrested shortly before _____ and by _____ the next morning, had been tried, _____ and sentenced to suffer on the _____.
7. Thanks to God for His _____ gift.
8. The _____, _____, _____ and _____ represented the _____ Jewish sects.
9. Father, _____ them for they _____ _____ what they do.
10. While hanging on the cross, Jesus exclaimed, "It is _____."

True or False

1. _____ Only twelve prophecies in the Old Testament speak of Christ.
2. _____ The blood-stained cross is the central theme of all the Bible.
3. _____ Peter carried the cross to Calvary for Christ.
4. _____ Jesus was on the cross for six hours.
5. _____ It is possible to crucify Christ again (Heb. 6:6).

Five Simple Questions

1. List the Old Testament scriptures that prophesy of Christ's birth, death, and resurrection.
2. Who carried the cross for Jesus?
3. How many sayings did Christ utter while on the cross? Name them.
4. What scripture states that the blood of Jesus was the purchase price for the church?
5. If not for Calvary, where would we be in eternity?

15

Plain Bible Talk

ABOUT THE SERIOUSNESS OF WORSHIP

PURPOSE
To come to understand how eternally serious it is to worship God.

GOAL
To learn how to worship and never consider any assembly as informal.

CHALLENGING THOUGHT
One can be at the right place and time, participate in all the proper outward acts of worship, and still not worship!

KEY WORDS

worship	truth	vain
ignorant	will	true
attitude	fear	respect

CHOICES BEFORE US
Either we will fear God and respect His way of worship or we will only go through the motions and worship as we desire.

THREE GREAT TRUTHS
God is to be worshiped.
He must be worshiped as He commands and with the right attitude.
Worship must be reverential.

SCRIPTURES TO BE READ AND STUDIED
Habakkuk 2:20   Psalm 29:1; 89:7; 95:6
Matthew 18:20   John 4:23–24
Revelation 22:9

PRAYER FOR TODAY
Dear God, when we come before Thee in worship,
help us to remember who we are, where we are,
what we are doing, and how we are doing it.

Introduction

Did you really worship when we last assembled? Answer: "Didn't you see me; I was here!" That is not the question. Read again our "Prayer for Today" and then read it again! One does not worship God accidentally. Worship is an act of reverence and it deserves and demands all our attention. Many have absolutely lost respect for the seriousness of worship. If you doubt this, take a look around when you assemble with the church. Our worship services often resemble a cage full of monkeys in the zoo, kindergartners in a romper room, a junior high outing at McDonalds, or public restrooms at Six Flags. Too many come to a place of worship but do not enter to worship. Worship is something you do, not something done to you. We must be reminded that Jehovah God is present, and our business with Him is serious! We approach the God of heaven when we gather to worship and the very purpose of worship is to honor and magnify the Almighty, not self. God determines the rules for worship and He fully expects us to abide by them. Each Christian should ask himself, "Did I really worship God today?" Brethren, what has happened to us? Do we no longer fear God? (Rom. 3:18). Do we no longer believe He means what He says? (Lev. 10:1–2). Have we now turned worship into parties and picnics? Sadly, many have done so.

Worship

One must prepare for worship, plan to worship, participate in worship, and respect what worship is. What many call worship is nothing short of sacrilege. We have rightly emphasized the truth concerning the acts of worship, but we often ignore the attitude of worship. Many modern "worship" activities are not acceptable to God (Mal. 1:6–14). Some think God will accept just anything. We do not do God a favor by worshiping; worship is for our benefit. Worship is attention, examination, memory, and paying homage to God. We truly stand on holy ground— God's presence—when we worship. If not, then let's break out the rook cards and sausage balls and have a party! When we refuse to participate and become a mere spectator, we do not engage in worship. The lax and casual attitude displayed by many is wrong. Worse still, it sends the wrong message to our youth. Many of them already think church is simply parties, chips, dip, pizzas, and a good time. Brethren are now talking about informal worship. For shame! Whether Wednesday night, Sunday night, or Sunday morning, worship is worship!

It Is a Matter of Respect

Out of respect, common courtesy, and decency, we do not drink a coke or eat a snack during a funeral or wedding. We remain quiet while in a library, we silence cell phone ringers and refrain from eating chips during a court session, and we are not in and out or up and down during our mother's funeral. Why then is it different when we gather to worship? If your child were lying in the casket, would you act the same as you do when in worship? Why not? Neither would we dress in the casual manner that we do in worship! Your answer is based on what you respect and do not respect! It is truly alarming to see the disrespect and lack of reverence for God and the risen Savior in our assemblies. It is little wonder that many exclaim, "Well, I did not get much out of worship today." We scream "bloody murder" when someone attempts to change an act of worship, as well we should. Yet, we continue to allow a lack of reverence to run rampant. I have seen brethren eat pizza, sandwiches, chips, cookies, candy, and doughnuts in the assembly. They have consumed coffee, tea, bottled water, and cokes. I have seen folks use tobacco in worship! Why did these things happen? No respect!

So This Is Worship!

It is time for worship to begin, and the assembly sounds like shoppers at the mall! So we begin and at least a dozen people are talking and laughing aloud. As we begin, the "picnic baskets" are opened. It sounds and looks like feeding time at the zoo. Immediately, four "worshipers" get up and go to the bathroom, five more get up, and no one knows why, and three more go to the bathroom. They smile, laugh, and wave at friends as they exit. Within ten minutes, twenty folks have looked at their watches. Two cell phones ring, several adults are popping gum and blowing bubbles, a family of eight is playing with the baby, a new teen convert stretches out in his pew and begins snoring, two males walk outside to make a lunch reservation, little Johnny has banged out thirteen verses of "Jingle Bells" by kicking the back of the pew, Suzie plays pitch with her friend using Daddy's keys, four more go the bathroom. ("Church of Christ" kids must have the worst kidneys in the world!) Six teenagers are passing notes during the Lord's supper, two small children have fussed and screamed for thirty-five minutes and the parents think it is so cute, twelve people leave after taking the Lord's supper and during the invitation, a host of folks get babies dressed, and the "picnic baskets" are organized as they get ready for the mad dash out. Where is the reverence?

Suggestions

1. Be silent and orderly and plan to worship. Focus on the blood-stained cross (Ps. 119:2).
2. Worship is something you do, not something done to you. Participate in worship (Ps. 95:6).
3. Focus, meditate, and realize what you are doing and who is present (Rev. 22:9).
4. Get a good night's sleep and prepare for worship (Ps. 122:1).
5. Pray for the congregation and thank God for the opportunity to worship Him (Ps. 99:5).
6. Bring your Bible so you can study and take notes during the teaching avenue of worship (Ps. 119:15).
7. Do not use worship time to clip nails, balance the checkbook, sleep, or play games (Hab. 2:20).
8. Allow God to be the object of worship and then worship in spirit and in truth (John 4:23–24).
9. Remember that worship is attention, memory, praise, fellowship, and service (Matt. 4:10).
10. Use the time God has given you to approach His holy throne with reverence and respect.

QUESTIONS

1. One can be at the right _____ and _____, _____ in the right items of worship, and yet still not _____.
2. Worship is an act of _____ and it deserves and _____ all our _____.
3. Worship is something you do, not something _____ to you.
4. One must _____ for worship, _____ to worship, _____ in worship and _____ what worship is.
5. Worship is _____, an _____, _____ and _____ homage to God.
6. When we become a _____ and not a _____, we are not worshiping.
7. Allow _____ to be the object of worship and then worship in _____ and in _____ (John 4:23–24).
8. Worship must be with fear and _____.
9. Have we now turned worship into _____ and_____?
10. What many call worship (and/or do in worship) is nothing short of _____.

TRUE OR FALSE

1. ____ God must be worshiped in the way He commands and with the right attitude.
2. ____ Reverence is a key factor in worshiping God.
3. ____ Worship can be in vain.
4. ____ One can accidentally worship God.
5. ____ The purpose of worship is to honor and magnify the Almighty.

FIVE SIMPLE QUESTIONS

1. Why is it impossible to give one's attention to a ball game and, at the same time, be worshiping God?
2. Why is serious worship a serious matter?
3. Do we worship to please God or to benefit ourselves? Defend your answer.
4. Why is it necessary to participate in worship?
5. Read Leviticus 10:1–2. How important is it to worship obediently?

16

ABOUT INSTRUMENTS IN WORSHIP

PURPOSE
To learn why the use of instrumental music in worship is sinful.

GOAL
To learn what God commands and will accept when we worship Him by singing.

CHALLENGING THOUGHT
No one can use an instrument of music in worship and remain in harmony with the truth of the New Testament.

KEY WORDS
sing	play	instrument
authority	worship	

CHOICES BEFORE US
Either we will respect and obey God by singing without instruments, or we will please ourselves by disregarding God's authority and use them.

THREE GREAT TRUTHS
God knows what is best.
He commanded us to worship Him in song without a mechanical instrument.
It is sin to use an instrument in worship to Him.

SCRIPTURES TO BE READ AND STUDIED

Acts 20:20, 27   1 Thessalonians 5:21
Revelation 22:18–19   Ephesians 5:19
John 14:15

PRAYER FOR TODAY

Dear God, help us have respect for all Thy holy commandments.

Introduction

We are told that some fifty percent of Christians do not know why the instrument should not be used, and twenty-five percent do not object to its being used! The beginning of the use of instruments in worship is well documented. Instruments were first introduced in AD 670. They caused such an uproar that they were taken out and not reintroduced until around AD 800. The New Testament does not lend any authority whatsoever to the use of instruments in worship. It is imperative that we teach each generation why instrumental music in worship is sinful. We must not use them if we have any desire to follow the pattern set forth in the New Testament. The only "instrument" we are to use is the heart—not the harp!

The Church of Christ Is Bound by New Testament Authority

Jesus built His church (Matt. 16:18). His church is subject to Him (Eph. 5:22–24). The New Testament is our complete and perfect guide (James 1:25; 2 Pet. 1:3; 2 John 9–11). The Old Testament has been taken out of the way (Col. 2:14–17; Heb. 10:9; Gal. 5:4).

The following is a complete list of all New Testament scriptures concerning music in worship: Matthew 26:30; Mark 14:26; Acts 16:25; Romans 15:9; 1 Corinthians 14:15; Ephesians 5:19; Colossians 3:16; Hebrews 2:12; and James 5:13. Each one teaches us to sing, and not once is mechanical music mentioned. Is this not reason enough to avoid using the instrument? Some brethren are now saying that they would not "push" for the use of the instrument, but neither would they oppose it! We must take a stand against its use.

What the Mechanical Instrument Does

The instrument rejects God's authority. It violates the principles of faith. It voids the very words of God. It violates specific commands. It voids an understanding of the Bible. It always leads to other things.

Here are some examples. One religious group brought in five hundred canary birds to sing praises to God. Another group brought in thirty-five canary birds to do the same thing. One group brought in trained seals that honked the tune of "Jesus Loves Me" on mechanical horns and then clapped for Jesus. One group played the "barking dog polka" and called it worship. Other groups now have barefoot dancers singing psalms. It is just as wrong to have mustard and chips for the Lord's supper as to have mechanical music in worship!

Feeble Defenses for the Use of the Instrument
1. *David used it.* He also practiced polygamy, offered animal sacrifices, and burned incense. Can we also do these things? The old law has been taken out of the way (Col. 2:14; Rom. 7:1–6). David is not the authority for our worship (Gal. 5:4).
2. *It develops talent.* So does dancing, swimming, and playing golf, but God is on His throne to rule, not as a judge for talent performances. Worship was never designed as a talent show. Read Colossians 3:17.
3. *What makes it right at home if it's wrong in worship?* We can do a multitude of things at home that we have no authority to do in worship. At home we bathe, cook, sleep, feed dogs, whistle, and watch TV, but none of these things constitute worship.
4. *There will be instruments in heaven.* Where does the Bible teach such? It is certainly not Revelation 5:8 and 14:12 ("as of" and "voices" of harpers). These represent the songs or singing in heaven. There will be no literal instruments in heaven. Anyway, what is done in heaven has no bearing on how we worship here on earth!
5. *The Bible does not say,* "Thou shalt not use mechanical music." Neither does the Bible say we cannot have ham and eggs for the Lord's supper, sing rock-and-roll songs in worship, baptize wart hogs, or beat our wives into next week. But God does tell us what He wants and how we are to treat people. When God told Noah to build

the ark of gopher wood (Gen. 6:14), that command eliminated pine, oak, and all other kinds of wood. (See lesson 4.) God simply tells us what He wants!

6. *The Greek word* psallo, *translated "make melody,"* means "to pluck or twang the bowstring." That is correct, but it also can be used to "touch the chords of the human heart," and that is how Paul used it in Ephesians 5:19. Paul tells us what instrument is to be plucked. If *psallo* means to touch the chords of a mechanical instrument, then every worshiper must play an instrument! Ephesians 5:19 does not command us to play a mechanical devise but to sing and make melody in our hearts. Psalm 98:5 shows the difference in playing and singing!

Conclusion

The Bible commands us to sing psalms, hymns, and spiritual songs by using the heart and lips. This is not only safe, but it is obeying God's specific commands. The performance of a choir, trio, or quartet, or the use of rock-and-roll songs or a mechanical instruments in worship is a sin because it violates what God commands. Why? We find no biblical authority for them.

QUESTIONS

1. No one can use a mechanical _____ in worship and remain in harmony with the New Testament.
2. God knows what is _____.
3. The only "instrument" we are to use is the _____ and not the _____.
4. The New Testament is our _____ and _____ guide.
5. It is just as wrong to have _____ and _____ for the Lord's supper as to have _____ ___ _____ in worship.
6. David is not the _____ for our worship.
7. There will be no _____ instruments in _____.
8. When God told Noah to build the ark out of _____ wood (Gen. 6:14), that eliminated _____ and all other trees.

9. Ephesians 5:19 says "sing," not "_____."
10. The Bible commands us to sing _____, _____ and _____ _____ songs by using the heart and _____.

TRUE OR FALSE

1. ____ The mechanical instrument of music was used in Christian worship in the first century worship.
2. ____ The Old Testament has been taken out of the way.
3. ____ The mechanical instrument of music rejects God's authority.
4. ____ Since one bathes at home, he can also bathe in worship.
5. ____ Psalm 98:5 shows the difference between playing and singing.

FIVE SIMPLE QUESTIONS

1. What scripture in the New Testament teaches that God authorizes vocal music for use in worship? What scripture in the New Testament teaches that God authorizes mechanical instruments for use in worship?
2. According to the New Testament, can mechanical instruments be used in worship to God? What is the only kind of music God has authorized for use in the church?
3. Must the church be subject to Christ? Give scriptural proof.
4. What three verses plainly teach that the Old Testament has been taken out of the way?
5. Does the Bible teach that literal instruments will be in heaven? Give reason for your answer.

17

Plain Bible Talk

ABOUT WHAT GRANNY WOULD HAVE SAID

PURPOSE
To return to the old paths so the home and church will be what God wants.

GOAL
To go back to yesteryear and re-learn basic and fundamental truths.

CHALLENGING THOUGHT
We sorely need to practice what our "godly" grandparents taught.

KEY WORDS

rules	respect	manners
fundamental	truth	home
church	God	no

CHOICES BEFORE US
Either we will honor and obey all that is right and decent, or we will walk the pathway of destroying the basic and fundamental truths of right and wrong.

THREE GREAT TRUTHS
The Bible is the absolute standard of truth.
Previous generations would be disgusted with present day immorality.
We must learn from the days of old.

SCRIPTURES TO BE READ AND STUDIED

Jeremiah 6:16	Job 8:8
Psalm 44:1; 71:18	2 Timothy 1:5; 3:15
Deuteronomy 32:7	

PRAYER FOR TODAY

Dear God, help us to remember Thee, Thy words, and the days of old.

Introduction

I wish everyone could have a grandmother like "Granny Pettus," my wife's grandmother. She is responsible for the conversion of many who are now faithful members of the church of Christ. She was the portrait of a real honest-to-goodness godly woman! I can still hear her words of wisdom, comfort, challenge, encouragement, and edification. She was a precious and sweet lady, and you never had to wonder about her love for truth and for the church. She taught the importance of basic and fundamental truths. Her work and general conduct were a tribute to her Maker, who must have been well pleased with her.

Remember When?

I can remember when folks, young and old, dressed, talked, and acted right! Character, integrity, and honesty were the norm, not the exception. Daddies were heads of homes, mothers were at home, and children were not ruling the home! Our nation, society, homes, and the church believed and practiced moral principles. We believed and taught that marriage came before babies; the bed was for married folks. God and the church came first and our priorities were right. We stood against homosexuality, abortion, and no-fault divorce. Preachers actually preached the Bible, named sin, and talked about hell. It was common to hear someone say, "That young-un needs a whooping." We tried to change people and not the church. We read, taught, and studied the Bible. The family knew when it was church time; there was no excuse not to go. We taught our children to work, to honor and obey their parents, to say "yes ma'am" and "no sir," to practice self-control, and to allow God, through the Bible, to control their minds. Yes, there was a time, but I am afraid many are at the point of no return concerning these matters.

How about you? Remember the three R's? Being triple dog dared? Modesty? Real reverent worship? "Church of Christ" referred to the real one and only church? Elders were actually appointed because they were biblically qualified? Children were seen and not heard? Preachers knew and preached the Bible and did not substitute "locker room pep talks" for sermons. Heretics were really disfellowshipped? We honored the flag?

What Granny Would Have Said and Taught Us

1. *Play fair.* Abiding by the rules was accepted and recognized (Phil. 3:16).
2. *There is a difference between boys and girls.* God made it that way. Homosexuality is sin! It is as dark as hell and as evil as Satan himself! (Rom. 1:26–32).
3. *That young'un needs a "whooping."* A word we knew personally! We need discipline at home, at church, and in our nation (Nah. 1:3).
4. *Learn to say I am sorry.* This did not make us thugs or wimps! (Luke 17:3–4).
5. *Take care of your "stuff."* Appreciate what God blesses you with (Matt. 6:33).
6. *Wash your ears.* The body is a gift from God. Take care of it (3 John 2).
7. *Clean up your mess.* Jesus wants us to be orderly (Mark 6:35–40).
8. *Learn to share.* God wants us to be a help to others (Matt. 28:18–20).
9. *Learn respect.* God, the Bible, the church, authority, others, and self deserve it (Job 32:6).
10. *It is wrong to steal, hit, and lie* (Matt. 7:12).
11. *Take care of things that belong to others* (1 Cor. 4:2).
12. *Honor your parents.* Obey, trust, and respect them (Matt. 15:4).
13. *Watch, hold hands, and stick together.* Why? Safety! (1 Pet. 1:22).
14. *The world is beautiful.* God made it so. Enjoy it! (Gen. 1:31).
15. *Think for yourself and take responsibility for your choices* (Gen. 3:12; 2 Cor. 5:10).
16. *There is a time to work and a time to play* (Prov. 24:30–34).

17. *Skunks stink!* There are some people, places, and things to avoid! (1 Cor. 15:33).

18. *Everything will be all right because God is in control* (Dan. 2:28; 3:17; 4:25).

19. *Be kind to others, especially the poor.* Never make fun of anyone (John 12:8).

20. *There are rules for everyone to follow* (John 14:15).

21. *God made the law of reproduction and it cannot be altered* (Gen. 1:12; 2:18–25).

22. *All in life is not fair, so get used to it* (Col. 3:1–2).

23. *Be good boys, girls, men, and women* (3 John 11).

24. *When problems come, pray, read the Bible, and attend church* (Matt. 11:28–30).

25. *When you say "I do," you really do.* Don't ever let the word *divorce* come out of your mouth (Matt. 19:1–9).

26. *"Young lady, you go back in your room and put some clothes on!"* (1 Tim. 2:8–15).

27. *"Young man, put on some decent clothes, get that ring out of your ear, get a hair cut, and don't even think about tattooing your body!"* (Lev. 19:28; Exod. 21:6; Rom. 12:1–2; 1 Pet. 4:3–4).

28. *Smoking and drinking are not "cool"* (1 Cor. 10:31).

29. *"You are not going to listen to that nasty music in this house"* (Ps. 101:3).

30. *"Before we eat, let's offer a prayer of thanksgiving"* (Eph. 5:20).

QUESTIONS

1. The Bible is the _____ standard of _____.
2. We must learn from the _____ of old.
3. In "days of old" preachers actually _____ the Bible.
4. Abiding by the _____ was accepted and recognized.
5. Learning to say "I am sorry" did not make us _____ or _____.
6. The _____ is beautiful, _____ made it so.
7. Think for _____ and take _____ for your choices.
8. There is a _____ to work and a _____ to play.
9. When problems come, _____, read the _____ and _____ church.
10. There are some _____, _____ and _____ to avoid.

TRUE OR FALSE

1. ____ Previous generations would be disgusted with present day immorality.
2. ____ Homosexuality is sin.
3. ____ God is in control of it all.
4. ____ Smoking and drinking are cool and are healthy for us.
5. ____ There are rules for everyone to follow.

FIVE SIMPLE QUESTIONS

1. How can we use ideas from the days of old to help us in our daily walk?
2. Should we try to change people to conform to the principles of Christ, or should we try to change His church to accommodate modern society? Defend your answer.
3. What does the principle laid down by the Golden Rule teach us about our relationship to another's possessions, person, and reputation? What then should be our view of stealing, hitting, and lying?
4. What are six things for which we must learn to have proper respect?
5. Since everything in life is not fair, what should be our attitude toward life?

18

Plain Bible Talk

ABOUT
SATAN'S HYDROPHOBIA

PURPOSE
To learn about the one "phobia" that terrifies Satan and all the demons in hell.

GOAL
To be reminded of and then teach the next generation about this phobia of Satan.

CHALLENGING THOUGHT
Satan will not and cannot ever be cured of this phobia (fear).

KEY WORDS

water	baptism	hell
defeat	fear	blood
remission	sins	

CHOICES BEFORE US
Either Satan has a morbid fear of water or he is delighted when a person is baptized.

THREE GREAT TRUTHS
Satan is terrified of water.
He can never overcome this fear.
We must "remind" him often of his hydrophobia.

SCRIPTURES TO BE READ AND STUDIED

Mark 16:16   Acts 2:38; 19:1–5
Romans 6:1–6   Galatians 3:26–27
James 2:19

PRAYER FOR TODAY
Dear God, give us courage to face Satan and remind him of baptism.

Introduction

Satan's hydrophobia (fear of water) is evident throughout the Bible. We will note some of the examples of his fears and conclude with baptism, the culmination of these phobias.

We live in a time when the religious world, and many of our own brethren, have dismissed baptism as being a part of God's plan of salvation. They are in support of Satan and his hydrophobia!

Baptism

Most of the religious world and some "gospel" preachers seem to think that Satan commanded baptism. Baptism is mentioned at least a hundred times in the New Testament. The Bible says that baptism will save (1 Pet. 3:21), put one into Christ (Gal. 3:27), add one to the church (Acts 2:38–47; 1 Cor. 12:13), wash away sins (Acts 22:16), and allow one to arise to a new life (Rom. 6:1–4). To reject baptism is to reject God (Luke 7:29–30). The Bible teaches that faith "kills" the love of sin, repentance "kills" the practice of sin, confession of Christ denounces sin, and baptism obtains the remission of sins. The reason Satan is so fearful of water is because it is used to baptize folks into Christ!

We know, of course, that baptism cannot in and of itself make one good, produce faith, erase temptation, make one religious, or "seal" one's salvation. Baptism is a command (Acts 10:48) and that should be sufficient in itself. God chose, commanded, and ordained baptism for the remission of sins. That forever settles the matter. Note the connection of baptism and the blood of Christ: Matthew 26:26–28 and Acts 2:38; Hebrews 9:14 and 1 Peter 3:21; Revelation 1:5 and Acts 22:16. It is by baptism that we contact the blood of Christ!

Four Ways to Read Mark 16:16

- *He that believeth and is baptized shall not be saved.* That is the atheist's teaching.
- *He that believeth not and is baptized shall be saved.* That is the doctrine for baptizing (sprinkling) babies.
- *He that believeth and is not baptized shall be saved.* That is the doctrine of faith only.
- *He that believeth and is baptized shall be saved.* That is the doctrine of the Bible!

Why Does Satan Have Hydrophobia?

1. Genesis 6–8. Satan's followers died in the flood. He must hate water!
2. Exodus 7:20. Water destroyed Satan's idol worship. The Nile River was a god to the Egyptians.
3. Exodus 14:26–31. Satan's servants were drowned by water. Just imagine Satan's rage.
4. Exodus 17:1–7. Satan's work and efforts to destroy God's people are defeated by water.
5. Exodus 32:15–20. Satan's worshipers were made to drink water which contained their god.
6. Joshua 4:8–14. Satan watched as God's people walked across the Jordan riverbed and into the promised land.
7. 1 Kings 18:25–40. Satan was totally embarrassed by water! His fear cannot be described by man.
8. 2 Kings 5:1–14. Satan was soundly "whipped" by the waters of Jordan. How he must despise water!
9. Mark 4:35–41. Jesus demonstrated that God is in control of Satan's phobia!
10. Mark 5:13–20. Once again Satan's workers faced defeat at the hand of water.
11. Mark 6:45–52. Jesus walked on water and demonstrated His power over Satan's phobia. Defeat again!
12. John 4:14; Revelation 22:17. God uses water to represent His eternal word. Satan is scared!

13. John 9:1–12. Water demonstrated God's miracles and also His power over Satan.
14. Acts 2:38–47. This is the culmination of Satan's hydrophobia (fear of water)!

Conclusion

The Bible teaches that baptism comes before salvation, remission of sins, eternal rejoicing, washing away of sins, new life, being in the one body, and the putting on of Christ. It is truly amazing how folks fight baptism. Again, many act as if Satan commanded baptism! The one baptism of Ephesus 4:5 is not John's; it is not of the Holy Spirit; it is not of fire. It is the one found in the great commission (Matt. 28:18–20). It is a burial in water (Acts 8:38; Rom. 6:3–4). It is for the remission of sins (Acts 2:38). There is no clearer way to demonstrate faith and respect for God than going down into water and being baptized for the remission of sins! Baptism is the "dividing line" between the church of Christ and every man-made religion. It is little wonder that Satan has hydrophobia!

Questions

1. Satan will not and _____ ever be cured of this _____ (fear).
2. _____ is terrified of _____.
3. _____ is mentioned at least _____ times in the New Testament.
4. _____ chose, _____ and _____ baptism for the _____ of sins.
5. It is by _____ that we contact the _____ of Christ!
6. He that _____ and is _____ shall be saved.
7. Satan's _____ died in the flood.
8. Jesus demonstrates that _____ is in control of Satan's _____!
9. Acts 2:38–47 is the_____ of Satan's _____ (_____ of _____).
10. The reason Satan is so fearful of _____ is because it is used to _____ folks into Christ!

True or False

1. ____ Baptism is a command of God.
2. ____ Baptism is for the remission of sins.
3. ____ Baptism puts one into Christ.
4. ____ Baptism is administered only to show that one is already saved.
5. ____ Mark 16:16, says, "He that believeth and is not baptized shall be saved."

Five Simple Questions

1. Concerning what subject must we often remind Satan?
2. What two things are connected in Revelation 1:5?
3. Since many do not believe God commanded baptism for the remission of sins, to whom must they attribute that plain teaching?
4. Did God ever use water to represent His eternal Word? Prove your answer with scripture.
5. Does scriptural baptism require a burial in water? Give scripture.

19

Plain Bible Talk

ABOUT BIBLICAL LOVE

PURPOSE
To allow the Bible to tell us what real Bible love is.

GOAL
To understand what biblical love is, and then put it into practice.

CHALLENGING THOUGHT
Jesus loves me this I know, for the Bible tell me so.

KEY WORDS

love	affection	God
world	obey	commandments
serve	Bible	

CHOICES BEFORE US
We will either love as God requires or develop a false love.

THREE GREAT TRUTHS
God is love.
We are to be a loving people.
Love demands obedience.

SCRIPTURES TO BE READ AND STUDIED
John 21:15–23; 3:16   Matthew 22:36–40
1 John 2:15–17; 3:18

Introduction

The word *love* is abused and misused. Everything from ice cream to ice hockey is "loved." There are four Greek words for the word love: *Agape* is God's love for us and how He wants us to feel toward Him. *Phileo* is the word for affection or friendship. *Storge* is the natural love for kinfolks. *Eros*, sexual love, is never used in the Bible. We all have the capacity and desire to love and be loved. Let us never forget to love God, family, church, brethren, neighbors, and even our enemies. But just what is involved in loving God and these people? Is it enough just say that we love them? No!

Love

Jesus asked Peter three times if he loved Him (John 21:15–23). The first two times He used a form of the non-emotional word for love, *agape*. The last time He used a form of the emotional affectionate word, *phileo*. (In that final question, Jesus was asking Peter if he had a warm, emotional, and affectionate love for Him, since he followed afar off and finally denied Him.) All three times Peter responded with *phileo*—he had affection for the Lord! Many Christians share Peter's feelings, but the kind of love Jesus wants is agape love; that is, love based on truth (1 John 2:5). It is proven by obedience (John 14:15). Agape love proves our discipleship. Agape love proves itself by doing (1 John 3:18).

Demonstrating Biblical Love

- *Your children.* Take time to love them. That is all they really want!
- *The unfaithful.* Call, write, visit, and pray for them.
- *The lost.* Love demands that we be concerned about their souls.
- *Your parents.* Tell and show them that you love them.
- *Your mate.* Allow every day to be a proving ground. Obedience (John 14:15). The gospel is God's demonstration of His love.
- *The faithful.* How we need to express and demonstrate this more! (John 13:34–35). We can do so by "feeding the birds." By this I mean doing the little everyday things that no one knows or sees. It is serving the Master "behind the scenes." Just as a wife serves

God by being the right kind of wife, we become true Christians by serving others. Do it for love!

- *Everyone.* The lonely, suffering, crippled, shut-in, sick, broken-hearted, widow, orphan, neighbor. Be there for them and be a Christian example (Zech. 8:23). When death invades a home, just be there and pray. Oh, you don't know what to say? Neither do I.

Do We Really Practice Biblical Love?

Read Ephesians 4:15 and Philippians 1:9. Paul tells us that Christians must teach in love. Love the truth to the extent that you tell others the whole truth, and true love will allow you to know truth from error. What a formula for every saint to follow!

Saying "I love you" seems to be the driving mindset of many Christians. If that is so important, then why is love not mentioned in the book of Acts? Did not Paul and Peter love those people? Yes, but they proved it by action and not with words. They were more concerned about saving souls with truth than saying, "Turn around and tell someone you love them!" Love people enough to tell them the truth—the whole truth. Half truths will not save.

Because I Love You

1. There is but one church for which our Lord died (Rom. 16:16; Acts 20:28).
2. Your parents are lost if they are not obedient to the gospel (Heb. 5:8–9).
3. You are lost unless you render obedience to God (Acts 2:38–47).
4. There is but one reason for divorce (Matt. 19:1–9).
5. Forsaking the assembly of the church is sin (Heb. 10:25–31).
6. Worship is serious and must be done God's way (John 4:23–24).
7. False teachers are liars and will be punished in hell (Isa. 56:9–11; Rev. 21:8).
8. Modern "versions" of the Bible, such as the New International Version, are dangerous (Rom. 16:18).
9. Hell is real, awful, and forever. Don't go to that agonizing place (Matt. 25:31–46).

10. Heaven is beautiful, precious, and worth it all (John 14:1–6).
11. Don't waste today; obey God. There are no changes after death (Luke 16:19–31).
12. The lost are really lost (2 Thess. 1:7–9). God will not change His law on judgment day.

QUESTIONS

1. _____ loves me this I know for the _____ tells me so.
2. Let us never forget to love _____, _____, _____, _____, _____ and even our _____.
3. Biblical _____ will produce its evidence by doing and not just _____ it (1 John 3:18).
4. The gospel is _____ demonstration of His love.
5. Love people enough to tell them the _____ and the _____ truth.
6. _____ truths will not save.
7. Heaven is _____, _____ and worth it all (John 14:1–6).
8. God is _____.
9. Just as a wife serves God by being the right kind of wife, we become true _____ by serving _____.
10. Concerning the lost, love demands that we be concerned about their _____.

TRUE OR FALSE

1. ____ The word *love* is not mentioned one time in the book of Acts.
2. ____ *Eros* is the love we are to have for God.
3. ____ There is but one church for which our Lord died.
4. ____ It is not important to prove our love, just say the words.
5. ____ The lost are really lost.

FIVE SIMPLE QUESTIONS

1. What are the four Greek words for love?
2. What will allow us to know truth from error?
3. In "Scriptures to Be Read and Studied," which teach us not to love the world.
4. Why would only foolish men wait until after death to obey God?
5. How many times did Jesus ask Peter if he loved Him?

20

Plain Bible Talk

ABOUT THE
IMPORTANCE OF NAMES

PURPOSE
To learn of the importance that God has placed on names.

GOAL
To honor the importance God has attached to names.

CHALLENGING THOUGHT
From the day of creation, God said names were important.

KEY WORDS

names	authority	Adam
Eve	division	unity
God		

CHOICES BEFORE US
Either we will honor God's authority and use scriptural names, or we will simply determine that we can make our own rules and believe that names do not really matter.

THREE GREAT TRUTHS
Names are important.
There is something in a name.
God said names were so important that He changed the names of certain people.

SCRIPTURES TO BE READ AND STUDIED

Genesis 2:19–20	Genesis 3:20–21; 5:2
Matthew 1:25	Proverbs 22:1; 17:5, 15
Acts 4:12	1 Peter 4:16

PRAYER FOR TODAY

Dear God, please help us to realize that names are important.

Introduction

From the beginning to the end of the Bible, God demonstrates the great importance of names. Even our authority is derived from the name of Christ (Col. 3:17). Yet multitudes disregard this and are teaching that there is nothing in a name or that it does not matter what name one wears as long as he is sincere. The name of Jesus is eternally important (Matt. 1:25; 3 John 7; 2 Tim. 2:19). Would one dare say that it is not? Why not, if there is nothing in a name?

Questions: Is a truck a fish? Is a pizza a skunk? Is an airplane a dog? Did Elvis Presley lead the children of Israel across the Red Sea? Take a look at the telephone book; are names not important? How much more so in religious matters?

Several years ago, a denominational preacher said, "Some people think the name is important. If you do not have a certain name, you will be lost. The name is not important. The church could be named Jack Rabbit. I would not want to name it that, but you could."

On judgment day, this "preacher" will know that names matter to God! If names do not matter, we would have absolute chaos in the world! The Bible condemns "Jack Rabbit" names in religion because they are unscriptural. Let's now study the importance of names.

1. *When identifying people, names are important.* Adam and Eve, not Mr. and Mrs. Jack Rabbit, were the first man and woman (Gen. 2:20; 3:20; 5:1–2). Noah, not Jack Rabbit, built the ark (Gen. 6). Mary, not Jack Rabbit, is the mother of Jesus (Matt. 1:18–25). God, not Jack Rabbit, made the heavens and the earth (Gen. 1:1). Jeremiah, not Jack Rabbit, was a prophet of God who penned the book of Jeremiah.

2. *When identifying places, names are important.* The four rivers of
the garden of Eden were Pison, Gihon, Hiddekel, and Euphrates (Gen.
2:10–14), not the Mississippi, Coosa, Tallapoosa, and Tennessee.
God destroyed the cities of Sodom and Gomorrah (Gen. 18:24), not
Oxford and Birmingham or Jack Rabbit and Cottontail. Jesus was
born in Bethlehem (Matt. 2:1), not Munford, Alabama, or Jack Rabbit City. Iraq is not America, and neither was Jesus crucified on
Bunker Hill.

3. *When identifying people, places, and things, names are important.*
John the Baptist ate locusts and wild honey (Matt. 3:4), not ham-
burgers and chips or jack rabbits. Jesus was crucified on a cross
(Matt. 27:32–61), not executed in an electric chair. Noah built an
ark (Gen. 6), not a Ford truck. Is a pencil the same thing as a bull
elephant?

4. *When identifying a family, names are important.* The Noah family,
not the Jack Rabbit family, survived in the ark (Gen. 6). How many
children do you know who are named Jack Rabbit, Old Skunk Face,
Ding Dong Head, Pencil Head, Saddam, Hitler, Judas, Fido, Spot, or
Satan? My wife wears my name, Butterworth, and not Hayes. Why?
She is married to me (Gen. 5:2). Four children were born into my
family and all are Butterworths. Names are important! Is calling on
God the same as calling on Satan?

5. *When identifying everyday things, names are important.* I shave
with a razor, not a jack rabbit. Wearing a crimson cap with the
University of Alabama's scripted A sewn on the front will not convince anyone that you are an Auburn fan. Calling me an atheist is
not the same as calling me a Christian. When ordering a pizza, do
you ask for swamp water and monkey meat? Is Wendy's the same as
McDonald's? Is a Ford the same as a Chevrolet? Is a Democrat the
same as a Republican? Is one name as good as another when it comes
to signing and cashing a check? Can you just sign it "Jack Rabbit"?

6. *When identifying the church, a name is important.* God did not call
the church Jack Rabbit! The church is the bride of Christ (Eph.
5:22–33). Jesus is her head (Col. 1:18). The wife does not wear the

name of the best man or some famous movie star. So it is with the church for which our Lord died (Acts 20:28). She does not wear denominational names. There is but one blood-bought church (Eph. 1:22–23; 4:4). The church is His house (1 Tim. 3:15). Salvation is in one name (Acts 4:12) and that name is not Jack Rabbit or any other name given by man. Those of God's house—His children—are called Christians (Acts 11:26) as was prophesied (Isa. 56:5; 62:2).

Conclusion

Jack Rabbit did not create the world, build the ark, or build the church. But God did direct His Son to build a church (Rom. 16:16). If that church can be called "Jack Rabbit" with God's approval, then Jack Rabbit must have purchased it with its blood! How eternally sad for one even to think that. Names were and are important to God, and they must be to us as well!

QUESTIONS

1. God said _____ were so important that He changed the names of certain people.
2. The name of _____ is eternally important.
3. When identifying people, _____ are important.
4. Adam and Eve (not _____ ____ ____ _____ _____) were the first man and woman.
5. There is something in a _____.
6. Is calling on God the same as calling on _____?
7. God never referred to His church by a denominational name, but He did refer to its local congregations as churches of _____ (Rom. 16:16).
8. There is but one name that will _____ (Acts 4:12).
9. If that church can be called "Jack Rabbit" with God's approval, then _____ _____ must have purchased it with its own _____!
10. The Bible condemns "Jack Rabbit" names in _____.

TRUE OR FALSE

1. ____ God said that names were not important.
2. ____ The Mississippi, Coosa, Tallapoosa, and Tennessee rivers are mentioned in the book of Genesis.
3. ____ All of God's children are in His family, the church.
4. ____ John the Baptist ate honey and wild ducks.
5. ____ One name is just as good as another.

FIVE SIMPLE QUESTIONS

1. By whose name is our authority derived?
2. What would result world-wide if appropriate names were not used?
3. What scripture teaches that Jesus is the head of the church?
4. What scripture in Genesis teaches that Eve was called "Mrs." Adam?
5. What would be the result of someone's teaching that Jesus was shot at Bunker Hill instead of having been crucified on Calvary?

21

Plain Bible Talk

ABOUT BEING STARS FOR GOD

PURPOSE

To learn what it takes to be a "star" for God and turn many to Him.

GOAL

To take a self-examination to see if I am a "star" for God (2 Cor. 13:5).

CHALLENGING THOUGHT

By shining like a star, I will turn many to God (Dan. 12:2–3).

KEY WORDS

star	shine	many
souls	salvation	influence
example	teach	

CHOICES BEFORE US

Either I will be God's person and shine like a star or my life will give Satan and his kingdom many more souls.

THREE GREAT TRUTHS

Being a star for God pleases Him.

Being a star means I will help bring about a spiritual resurrection in the church.

The lost are really and truly lost!

SCRIPTURES TO BE READ AND STUDIED
Daniel 12:2–3   2 Corinthians 13:5
Zechariah 8:23   Luke 6:26
Proverbs 11:30

PRAYER FOR TODAY
Dear God, help me to be Thy "star" and turn many to Thee.

Introduction

Daniel challenged the Jews to be God's people and to become stars after the Babylonian captivity (Dan. 12:1–4). He told them they were responsible to bring about a spiritual resurrection. The resurrection in these verses is not the one, great general resurrection when all will arise (John 5:28–29). Rather, it is a spiritual resurrection for God's people (Dan. 12:2).

The book of Daniel provides us with an outline of what it means to be a star for God (Rom. 15:4). We stand in dire need of a spiritual revival in the church of Christ as never before! Daniel challenged the Jews that if they would stand with God, do His work, and obey Him, they would shine as stars, turn many to Him, and bring about a spiritual resurrection (Dan. 12:2–3). What a challenging and thought-provoking statement! If the church fails to accomplish this, it has no one to blame but itself. Every Christian should be interested in what it takes to be a star for God. Just think: God said I would shine forever if I would do my part to bring about a spiritual resurrection!

Daniel Tells Us How

- Outlive the world (1:8).
- There is a God in heaven (2:28).
- Put God first (3:1).
- Get rid of pride (4:29).
- Everything we have comes from God (5:23).
- Prayer is essential (6:10).
- There is a judgment day (7:10).
- Fear and respect God and His word (8:27).

- Confess that we have failed to be stars (9:4–5).
- The Bible can be understood (10:14).
- The Bible is God's holy words (11:28).
- Souls are at stake (12:1–4).

Examine Yourself to Determine if You Are a Star

1. Do I love God with all my heart and more than anything or anyone? (Matt. 10:37) _____
2. Have I been baptized for the remission of my sins? (Acts 2:38; 22:16; 1 Pet. 3:21) _____
3. Do I attend every service possible? (Heb. 10:25; 1 Cor. 4:2) _____
4. Do I study my Bible every day? (2 Tim. 2:15; 2 Pet. 3:18) _____
5. Do I pray daily for elders, deacons, members, and the lost? (1 Thess. 5:17; Matt. 6:6–15) _____
6. Am I living, dressing, talking, and acting better than non-Christians? (1 Pet. 3:4) _____
7. Am I sincere and reverent in worship? (Matt. 18:20; John 4:24) _____
8. Do I really want to go to heaven? (John 14:1–6) _____
9. Am I now trying to save a soul because I believe the lost are really lost? (Prov. 11:30; James 5:19–20) _____
10. Do I leave my Christianity in the church building when I leave worship? (1 John 3:18) _____
11. Do I sincerely want the congregation to grow? (1 Cor. 14:12) _____
12. Will I commit myself to work, pray, give, and support the local church? (1 Cor. 14:12) _____
13. Do I really love the local congregation—its elders, deacons, evangelists, teachers—all members? (1 Pet. 2:17) _____
14. Am I interested in having a home Bible study with someone? (2 Tim. 2:2) _____
15. Do I visit the nursing homes, shut-ins, sick, weak members, and others who need me? (Matt. 25:35–40) _____
16. Do I keep a prayer list and pray for others every day? (1 Thess. 5:17) _____

17. Have I called, visited, or checked on my brethren who are absent? (James 4:17) _____
18. Have I invited someone to church this week? (John 1:42) _____
19. Have I recently given someone a tract or told someone about the Master? (Luke 14:23) _____
20. Do I visit the hospitals, send cards to the sick, and encourage others? (Matt. 5:47) _____
21. Will I begin doing my part to bring about a spiritual revival in the congregation where I worship? ___

QUESTIONS

1. By shining like a star, I will turn many to _____.
2. The lost are really and truly _____.
3. Every Christian should be interested in what it takes to be a _____ for _____.
4. There is a _____ in heaven.
5. The Bible is _____ holy _____.
6. Am I _____, _____, _____ and acting better than non-Christians?
7. Will I begin doing my _____ to bring about a _____ revival in this congregation?
8. Do I love _____ with all my _____ and more than anything or _____?
9. Do I really want to go to _____?
10. I will either be God's _____ and shine like a "star" or my life will give _____ and his kingdom many more _____.

TRUE OR FALSE

1. ___ Daniel 12:2–3 is discussing the great resurrection found in John 5:28–29.
2. ___ Daniel 12:2–3 is discussing a spiritual resurrection for God's people.
3. ___ The Bible can be understood.
4. ___ Each person should take a self-examination to see if he is a star for God.
5. ___ If the church fails to bring about a spiritual resurrection, it can blame the prophets.

FIVE SIMPLE QUESTIONS

1. What verse says a person who wins souls is wise?
2. What verse teaches that one should not desire that all men speak well of them?
3. What verse teaches that stewards of God are to be found faithful?
4. What verse teaches us to love in deed and truth, and not with words only?
5. What verse teaches us to study the Bible?

22

Plain Bible Talk

ABOUT GOING BEYOND WHAT IS WRITTEN

PURPOSE
To find out what God does and does not allow.

GOAL
To do only what the Bible allows, neither going beyond nor falling short of it.

CHALLENGING THOUGHT
I must honor God's generic and specific commands.

KEY WORDS

authority	generic	specific
beyond	add	subtract
err	knowledge	

CHOICES BEFORE US
Either we will do all things God's way or we will walk by our own rules.

THREE GREAT TRUTHS
God means what He says.
He knows what is best for us.
We sin by not knowing the Scriptures.

SCRIPTURES TO BE READ AND STUDIED

Matthew 22:29	Hosea 4:6
Jeremiah 6:16; 18:15	Jeremiah 44:16
1 Corinthians 4:6	Revelation 22:18–19
Mark 10:21	John 10:35

PRAYER FOR TODAY

Dear God, give us courage to always do what Thou hast commanded.

Introduction

The one true great God has made plain what He expects of us. His command to do one thing excludes the doing of all else. Just as I give someone my telephone number without telling him to exclude every other number in the telephone book, God so instructs us. If your wife or mother sends you to the store for a quart of milk, does she have to list everything she does not want? When God specifies a thing, He does not give an option or make it multiple choice! We must honor these matters.

Examples from Bible Characters

Adam and Eve knew God's specific command (Gen. 3:2–3). Moses knew God's specific command (Num. 20:1–13; Deut. 1:37). Uzzah knew the command of God (2 Sam. 6:7). The young prophet knew exactly what God allowed and did not allow (1 Kings 13:9, 11, 18, 24). Nadab and Abihu also knew God's specific command (Lev. 10:1–3). What if the Jews had offered a black heifer instead of a red one? (Num. 19:1–10). What if they had offered a red blemished one? A white one? These serve as reminders that God specified, and He meant what He said! (Rom. 15:4). Oh, how I pray that everybody, including my brethren, would accept this truth! When anyone rejects doing what God has commanded and authorized, that person is in essence saying he knows a better way than God's way! If not, then exactly what is he saying? Read Romans 3:18 and Psalm 119:6. We must teach others to leave their junk—man-made beliefs—in the world and not bring it into the church!

Obeying God's Generic and Specific Commands

1. *God said to worship (generic command).* Had He left it at that, we could worship idols or whatever we wished. But God said, "Worship me" (specific) (Rev. 22:9) and that eliminates all else! It is senseless, foolish, and unbiblical to ask where God says not to worship Hobo the frog or Buddha. When He told us to worship Him, He was saying, "Thou shalt not worship Buddha."

2. *God said to give (generic command).* Had He left it at that, one could give dirt, leaves, or rocks. But God said to give on Sunday as we have been financially prospered (specific) (1 Cor. 16:1–2). So God did say, "Thou shalt not give me dirt or leaves on Sunday."

3. *God said to marry (generic).* Had He left it at that, one could marry his car or dog, and he could have ten wives. Homosexuals could form same-sex marriages. But God said one man and one woman should marry (specific) (Gen. 2:18–25; Matt. 19:1–9). God most certainly did say, "Thou shalt not marry your car" and "A man shall not marry another man."

4. *God said to have music when we worship (generic).* Had He left it at that, we could worship Him with vocal or instrumental music, sing rock songs, or chant football fight songs. But God said to sing psalms, hymns, and spiritual songs with the heart (specific) (Eph. 5:18–19). God did say, "Thou shalt not sing rock songs" and "thou shalt not use a piano."

5. *God told Noah to build the ark of wood (generic).* Had He left it at that, Noah could have used pine or oak. But God said to build it out of gopher wood (specific), and that eliminated all other kinds of wood! (Gen. 6:14). God did say, "Thou shalt not use pine."

6. *God said to use a name in religion (generic).* Had He left it at that, one could choose any name: Elmer Fudd, Popeye, or Elvis. But God said to wear the name "Christian" (specific) (Acts 11:26; Acts 4:12). God did say, "Thou shalt not wear any man's name."

7. *God said to be a member of a church (generic).* Had He left it at that, one could choose from several thousand churches, but those who are being saved are baptized into the one body, the body of Christ

(specific) (Matt. 16:18; Acts 20:28; Rom. 16:16). God did say, "Thou shalt not take the church of your choice."

8. *God told Naaman to dip in water (generic).* Had God left it at that, Naaman could have dipped one time in any creek, lake, or river. But God said dip seven times in the Jordan River (specific) (2 Kings 5:10). God did say, "Thou shalt not dip seven times in the Nile River."

9. *God said for us to eat a supper in worship (generic).* Had He left it at that, one could choose Monday and eat peas and goat meat. But God said to partake of unleavened bread and fruit of the vine (specific) on Sunday (Matt. 26:26–28; Acts 20:7). God most certainly did say, "Thou shalt not eat peas and goat meat for the Lord's supper."

10. *God said to be baptized (generic).* Had He left it at that, one could be baptized in oil because he was already saved. But God said to be baptized in water to be saved (specific) (Acts 8:36–39; 1 Pet. 3:21; Acts 2:38). God did say, "Thou shalt not be baptized in oil."

QUESTIONS

1. We _____ by not knowing the _____.
2. The commanding to do one _____, excludes the doing of all _____.
3. When God specifies a thing, He does not give us an _____ or a multiple _____!
4. God said one _____ and one _____ should marry.
5. God said to sing _____, _____ and spiritual _____ with the heart.
6. God told Noah to build the ark out of _____ wood.
7. God said to wear the name _____.
8. God told Naaman to dip _____ times in the _____ _____.
9. God said to partake of the Lord's supper on _____.
10. The Lord's supper is _____ bread and fruit of the _____.

TRUE OR FALSE

1. ____ Uzzah was ignorant of God's commands.
2. ____ Unless God tells us every specific to do, we can choose whatever pleases us.
3. ____ Hosea 4:6 says God's people are saved through ignorance of His word.
4. ____ When God commanded us to worship Him, that eliminated our choice to worship an idol instead.
5. ____ God said that one must be baptized in water to be saved.

FIVE SIMPLE QUESTIONS

1. Should we honor God's generic or His specific commands? Give reason for your answer.
2. What color was the heifer to be that God commanded the Jews to offer? (Num. 19:1–10).
3. What are folks really saying when they refuse to do what God has commanded and authorized?
4. What verse tells us not to go beyond the Scriptures?
5. What verse commands us to partake of the Lord's supper on the first day of the week?

23

Plain Bible Talk

ABOUT HUMAN SUFFERING

PURPOSE
To see from the Bible why we suffer.

GOAL
To understand suffering, how to accept it, and then how to deal with it.

CHALLENGING THOUGHT
We must not blame God for all the suffering we experience!

KEY WORDS

suffer	grieve	sin
choice	ignorance	law
freedom	faith	character

CHOICES BEFORE US
Either the Bible is right or God is to blame for all suffering.

THREE GREAT TRUTHS
We will never fully understand suffering.
There is value to suffering.
Suffering is a part of the life cycle.

SCRIPTURES TO BE READ AND STUDIED

Isaiah 38:5	Romans 14:7
Romans 8:17	Job 23:10
Psalm 119:71	Exodus 20:5

Prayer for Today
Dear God, help us to be strong when our world falls apart.

Introduction

God grieved (Ps. 78:40). Jesus grieved (John 11:35; Mark 3:5). The Holy Spirit grieved (Eph. 4:30). Inspired men grieved (Ps. 119:136). As human beings, we also will grieve and suffer (Job. 14:1). If God promised exemption from suffering, some would serve Him for the wrong reason. Suffering is a part of life and is one of the most puzzling problems of the human mind. Why does God allow suffering? Why did my mother, sister, or husband have to suffer so? We need help from the Almighty if we are to answer these questions. Always remember that God hears our prayers and sees our tears (Isa. 38:5). In Judges 6 the people of God were suffering from enemy attacks, and their property was being destroyed. Many were dying, and some of those who escaped were living in caves. Why? They had made wrong choices! (Read the first part of the chapter.)

Not Everything That Happens Is God's Will

Three times in the book of Jeremiah (7:31; 19:5; 32:35) God said His people were doing things that had not entered His mind. God has chosen to avoid a knowledge of some things, and these verses prove that. God made man upright, but man seeks out many ways to sin (Eccles. 7:29). Satan is at work. He is very active in opposing the good and the right, and he influences people (Job 1:6–7; 2 Cor. 11:4; 1 Pet. 5:8; Luke 22:31). So do not blame God for every bad thing that happens. Good can come from every disaster (Rom. 8:28).

We Suffer Because

1. *The devil is at work* (1 Pet. 5:8). Read the last paragraph again. It is not God's fault!
2. *We break God's natural laws* (Gen. 1:31). A head-on collision with a semi will bring suffering. So will falling off a ten-story building or picking up a live 880-volt power line. What will happen to a man who drinks a glass of gasoline, Drano, or sulfuric acid? The laws of nature say he will die! I can pray "till the cows come home" after I

drink a pint of diesel fuel, but I am going to suffer! That is not God's fault!

3. *We make wrong choices* (Isa. 7:15; Deut. 30:15, 19, 20). We are not robots that must serve God whether or not we choose to do so! We are beings who have freedom of choice. A man may choose to drink whiskey and develop liver disease. Whose fault is it when he suffers? His or God's? It is of the man's choosing! Whose fault is it when a man robs a bank and, as a result, is sentenced to prison, sodomized, and killed by a fellow inmate? His! Whose fault is it when a man chooses to be a homosexual, contracts AIDS, and dies a horrible death? His! It is not God's fault! (Gal. 6:7; Ezek. 18:32).

4. *We abuse our freedom* (2 Kings 17:7–18). Judah in Babylonian captivity is a prime example of abusing freedom. Another example is the suffering brought upon families because of war. Just look at all the suffering that innocent people endured during the flood, the Babylonian captivity, the destruction of Jerusalem, our own Civil War, the Vietnam war, and myriads of other disasters. Nations that abuse their freedom will cause much suffering. It is not God's fault!

5. *We choose to be in ignorance* (Rom. 12:1–2; 1 Cor. 3:16–17; 10:31; 3 John 2). When one uses tobacco, alcohol, and other drugs, he will suffer. The one who is gasping for breath because of smoking has no one to blame but himself. The person who plays with rattlesnakes will suffer. A man who lies with a prostitute is unwise and sinful. He is likely to suffer from her diseases. A man who plays Russian roulette and blows his brains out didn't weigh the consequences. Both he and his family will suffer. Abortion! It is not God's fault!

6. *We possess a lack of faith in God* (Acts 27:25). Because we lack courage, fear, respect, and faith in God and His Word, we suffer. Israel did until David stepped up (1 Sam. 17). The people before the flood did until Noah stepped up (Gen. 6:8, 22). Until we "step up" and believe God, both we and our families will suffer at the hands of ungodly powers. There is a God; He rules and He will deliver (Dan. 2:28; 3:17; 4:25). Do we really believe that? God has done all He will do. Our lack of faith is not God's fault!

7. *We live on earth with other human beings* (Rom. 14:7; Exod. 23:2; Num. 32:23). The innocent suffer daily because of abandonment, drunk drivers, and disease. The little children, during the forty years of wandering in the wilderness, are examples of this. It is not God's fault!

8. *God would have to change His will, His law, and His promises to stop suffering* (Gen. 2:17; Rom. 5:12–15). Note Psalm 119:89; Matthew 24:35; Jude 3; and John 12:48. God will not stop suffering—He will not, He cannot do so (Num. 23:19; Mal. 3:6). Suffering is not God's fault!

Conclusion

Suffering will build character, lead some to Christ, cause us to yearn for heaven, and instill sympathy toward others. It will teach us how to pray. Suffering will increase our goodness and humility, counter and silence the enemies of the cross, and help us to be more appreciative. It will also help us to be thankful for life and dependent on God. Suffering will keep us from becoming content and satisfied with this old world and will help us to know that the only thing that really matters is dying in the Lord.

Yes, many times the innocent suffer along with the guilty; human suffering is still not fully understood, but this I know: one day when I cross those chilly waters, there will be no more suffering! Just one glimpse of Jesus coming in glory will make all the suffering, trials, and heart-aches worthwhile.

QUESTIONS

1. We must not blame _____ for all the _____ we experience.
2. _____ is a part of the life cycle.
3. God made _____ upright, but man seeks out many ways to _____ (Eccles. 7:29).
4. Out of every disaster, there can be _____ to come from it.
5. The _____ is at work (1 Pet. 5:8).
6. Man is not a _____ that serves _____ whether he wants to or not.
7. When one uses _____, drugs, or alcohol he will _____.
8. God would have to change His _____, _____ and _____ to stop suffering.
9. Yes, many times the _____ suffers along with the evil.
10. Just one _____ of Jesus coming in _____ will make all the _____, _____ and _____ worthwhile!

TRUE OR FALSE

1. ____ It is impossible for man to grieve God, the Holy Spirit, or Christ.
2. ____ Everything that happens is God's fault.
3. ____ Man sometimes suffers because he makes wrong or bad choices.
4. ____ If God promised exemption from suffering, some would serve Him for the wrong reason.
5. ____ According to Isaiah 38:5, God hears our prayers and sees our tears.

FIVE SIMPLE QUESTIONS

1. Why is it difficult for us to understand human suffering?
2. How many times does the book of Jeremiah state that people were doing things that had not entered God's mind?
3. What verse teaches that our sins will find us out?
4. What two verses can be given to prove that Jesus cried (grieved)?
5. What chapter in the book of Judges teaches that people were suffering because they had made wrong choices?

24

Plain Bible Talk

ABOUT WHY THERE ARE SO MANY CHURCHES

PURPOSE
To learn the origin of man-made churches.

GOAL
To learn why men were not satisfied with the one true blood-bought church.

CHALLENGING THOUGHT
No denominational church has a biblical right to exist!

KEY WORDS

one	apostasy	blood
purposed	seed	truth
sow	body	head
church		

CHOICES BEFORE US
Either the church of Christ or man-made churches are wrong; both cannot be right!

THREE GREAT TRUTHS
There is only one true church.
Our religious neighbors must see a difference between us and them.
We will reap what we sow.

SCRIPTURES TO BE READ AND STUDIED
Matthew 16:18   Acts 20:28; 2:38–47
Romans 16:16   Ephesians 1:22–23; 4:4

PRAYER FOR TODAY
Dear God, we thank Thee so much for the church of Christ.

There Is Only One True Church

In the days of the apostles, there was but one church (Eph. 4:4; Col. 1:18). That is the way God planned it, and man cannot change that fact! We should want our neighbors to know this, as well as our brethren! If I had only one lesson to teach or preach, this would be the one. How in the world did we go from one church to several thousand? Some now estimate that there are from twenty thousand to forty thousand sects in the United States. Revelation 22:18–19 provides the answer! Respecting biblical authority will cause us to accept God's truth about this. If Jesus died for only one church, why do we need others? We do not!

That One Church of the Bible

- It was purposed before the foundation of the world (Eph. 3:9–11).
- It was foretold by God's prophets (Isa. 2:1–4; Dan. 2:44).
- It was promised by Jesus Himself (Matt. 16:18; Mark 9:1).
- It was prepared by God's servants (Matt. 3:1–3; 18:15–17).
- It was perfected (became a reality) (Acts 2:37–47).
- It was the church to which all the saved in the New Testament were added (Acts 2:47).
- It was purchased by the blood of Christ (Acts 20:28).
- It was established in Jerusalem, in AD 33 (Acts 2:1–47).
- It was built to honor Christ (Rom. 16:16; Acts 4:12).
- It is the one body (Eph. 1:22–23; 4:4).

Which One?

Again, there is but one (Eph. 4:4–6). God did not give us a choice! What would you think of the people in Noah's day asking which ark, or the Jews asking which temple, or our asking which God? What part of one do we not understand? One means one, not two or ten thousand! There is one head and one body (Col. 1:18). That one church satisfied God; why not men?

Apostasy and Man-made Churches

Warnings of apostasy were given (Matt. 7:15–27; Acts 20:28–30; 2 Tim. 4:3–4). Man became dissatisfied with the one blood-bought church and started other churches.

- Catholic (AD 606 in Rome, by Rome).
- Lutheran (1517 in Germany, by Martin Luther).
- Church of England (1534 in England, by Henry VIII).
- Presbyterian (1536 in Geneva, Switzerland, by John Calvin).
- Baptist (1609 in Amsterdam, Holland, by John Smyth).
- Baptist in America (1639 in Providence, Rhode Island, by Roger Williams).
- Methodist (1729 in England, by John Wesley).
- Mormon, LDS (1830 in New York, by Joseph Smith).
- Adventist (1831 in New York, by William Miller).
- Jehovah's Witness (1844 in Pittsburgh, by Charles Russell).
- Salvation Army (1865 in London, by William Booth).
- Church of God (1886 in Cleveland, Tennessee, by Richard Spurling).

Note that each of these man-made churches has a different founder, name, date of origin, place of origin, plan of salvation, and doctrine. Martin Luther began what is called the Reformation Movement. He wanted to reform the Roman Catholic Church! Later, Alexander Campbell, Barton Stone, and many others made an effort to return to the Bible and the one church. Their work, founded on a return to the Bible, became known as the Restoration Movement (John 18:34).

We Reap What We Sow

The Bible plainly teaches the sowing-and-reaping principle, whether in the physical or spiritual realm (Gen. 1:11–12; Luke 8:11; Matt. 13:38; Gal. 6:7). There are no exceptions! No one plants corn so he can reap grapes. No farmer believes he can plant okra seed and reap cotton! Why? Because God's laws don't work that way (Gen. 1:11–12). Can one produce a goat by breeding a skunk with an elephant? Two goats will produce a goat! One must plant corn to get corn; peas to get peas; squash to get squash. If not, please prove this wrong. Note Matthew 7:16; James 3:12; and Galatians 6:7.

The Principle of Genesis 1:11–12; Luke 8:11;
Matthew 13:38; and John 15:5–6

The Bible is God's seed. The human heart is the field. What the branches produce is determined by the vine (or plant). This is just as true in the spiritual realm! Question: Can one plant a single kernel of corn and grow a single plant that can produce okra, wheat, corn, apples, oranges, tomatoes, cucumbers, peas, and watermelons? Of course not! Why? Because that would violate natural law! Then why does the religious world teach that one can plant God's seed—the Bible (Luke 8:11)—into the field, the hearts of men (Matt. 13:38), and come up with a thousand different plants, churches of men? (Matt. 15:13). Can the Bible planted in the hearts of men produce Catholics, Baptists, Methodists, and Mormons? No! Why not? To get Mormons, one must plant Mormon seed (doctrine). To get Baptists, one must plant Baptist seed! Planting their seed is the only way to produce them! Why? Because God said so! Whom do you believe, God or man? I believe God.

QUESTIONS

1. No _____ church has a _____ right to exist!
2. In the days of the _____, there was but _____ church.
3. There is one _____ and one _____ (Col. 1:18).
4. Note that each of these _____ _____ churches has a different _____, _____ of origin, _____ of salvation, and _____.
5. The Bible plainly teaches that one _____ what he sows, whether in the _____ or _____ realm.
6. No one can plant corn and reap _____.
7. The _____ is God's seed.
8. The _____ heart is the _____ in which the seed (Bible) is to be planted.
9. To get Mormons, one must plant _____ seed (doctrine), and to get Baptists, one must plant _____ seed (doctrine)!
10. Respecting biblical _____ will cause us to accept _____ truth about this.

TRUE OR FALSE

1. ____ God purposed before the foundation of the world to give us the church.
2. ____ The one church of the Bible was established in Jerusalem, in the year AD 33.
3. ____ This one church was purchased by the blood of good men.
4. ____ It is possible to plant okra seed and reap apples.
5. ____ John Calvin established the church of Christ.

FIVE SIMPLE QUESTIONS

1. What verse states that Jesus purchased the church with His own blood?
2. What verse states there is but one body?
3. What verse says one will reap what he has sown?
4. What verse in the Old Testament says that every seed will produce after its own kind?
5. What verse teaches that God's Word is the seed?

25

Plain Bible Talk

ABOUT THE
RELIGION OF ISLAM

PURPOSE
To learn more about the Islamic religion.

GOAL
To present a brief outline of this false religion.

CHALLENGING THOUGHT
If the Quran (Koran) is right, then Jesus is a liar.

KEY WORDS

Bible	Jesus	truth
Quran	false	Muhammad
God	Allah	

CHOICES BEFORE US
Either the Bible or the Quran is wrong; both cannot
be right.

THREE GREAT TRUTHS
Jesus is God's only begotten Son.
Jesus' teachings are all divine and true.
Muhammad is a false prophet.

SCRIPTURES TO BE READ AND STUDIED

Proverbs 30:6	Ecclesiastes 3:14
Jude 3	Revelation 22:18–19
John 12:48; 17:17	

PRAYER FOR TODAY
Dear God, we thank Thee for being the one and only God.

Muhammad, the False Prophet

Muhammad was born in AD 570 in Mecca, Arabia, now Saudi Arabia. He was a poor orphan but married a rich widow in AD 595. He had at least fifteen wives. When his first wife died, he married a nine-year-old girl!

As a child, he began to have seizures and came to believe that God was communicating with him because of these seizures. He then claimed he had a vision of Gabriel and was convinced that he was a prophet of God. He stated that he believed that Jesus and the biblical prophets were divine, but their teachings had been distorted, and his teachings superseded theirs. In other words, his teachings were superior to Christ's! He fled to what is now Medina when his life was threatened by Ishmael's descendents, the Arabs, but later he converted many of them. He quickly gained power and captured Mecca. He then destroyed the idols with the exception of the "Black Stone," which he claimed had come from heaven. Muhammad believed that Abraham had placed the stone where it was located. Mecca became the religious center of Arabia. Muhammad died in AD 632 at the age of 62, He left behind a collection of his "revelations," which became a part of the Quran. The following is a summary of Islam.

The Wrongs of Islam

- It carries the wrong name (Islam, Muslim, Moslem).
- It has the wrong founder (Muhammad).
- It began at the wrong date (AD 622).
- It began at the wrong place (Mecca).
- It has a wrong way to worship (Muhammad).
- It has the wrong requirements to be saved (no obedience to the gospel).
- It has the wrong standard (Quran).
- It denies that Jesus died on the cross.

- It denies that Jesus is the Son of God.
- It denies the godhead.

In short, the Quran is a collection of mishmash. It is not inspired!

Other Wrongs of Islam and the Quran

Islam is not a peaceful religion! In order to go to heaven, the followers of Allah are to kill all non-believers and infidels—those not of their faith. And that includes us! Jihad is an Islamic holy war, and even though the Arabic word *Allah* is translated God, Islam's Allah and our Jehovah are not the same! Allah was the name of the moon-god that preceded Islamic Arabian people. The Allah of the Quran is as different from Jehovah God as gorillas are from apples!

A general summation of Islam is covered in their Five Pillars of Faith:

- Repeating the creed: "There is no God but Allah, and Muhammad is the prophet of Allah."
- Daily prayer: Five times a day.
- Almsgiving: Share with the needy and poor.
- Fasting: No food or drink during daylight hours during the month of Ramadan.
- The Pilgrimage: At least one pilgrimage to Mecca in their lifetime.

To become a Muslim, one must:
- Believe in Allah as the one true God.
- Believe that angels are the tools of God's will.
- Believe in the four inspired books: The Torah of Moses, the Psalms of David, the Gospel of Jesus, and the Quran. (Muslims believe the first three in this list are corrupt, so the Quran is superior.)
- Believe in the twenty-eight prophets of Allah, of whom Muhammad is the last.
- Believe in a final day of judgment.

Sad and Ridiculous Verses from the Quran

1. Surah 4:157. Jesus was neither killed nor crucified.

2. Surah 9:30. Jesus is not the Son of God.

3. Surah 4:171. There is no such thing as the godhead.

4. Surah 4:34. Women can be admonished and then beaten.

5. Surah 4:3. Men can have as many as four wives, but women cannot have multiple husbands.

6. Surah 9:5; 5:33. Violence, harm, and death should be upon the non-Muslims.

7. Surah 2:228, 282. Men are superior to women because women are less intelligent.

Conclusion

The so-called revelations that Muhammad had were no more than his imagination playing tricks on him. Muhammad is revered more highly—by more than a billion followers—than Christ! The word *Islam* is Arabic meaning "submission," not peace, as many claim. The word *Muslim* is a form of the word *Islam* and means "one who submits." Never fall for the guise that this false religion is peaceful and that it serves the same one, true, great God that Christians worship! (Isa. 45:5). Islam denies that Jesus is who He claims to be! Also, remember the bombings that have taken place during recent years, and the many lives lost in those awful, horrible, terrible, and vicious attacks in the name of their "peaceful religion"! Give me a break! This false religion promotes hate and death.

Yes, as an American citizen, I am concerned. As Christians we must stand against Islam and, with the sword of the Spirit, defend God, His only begotten Son, the gospel, and the blood-bought church! What say ye?

QUESTIONS

1. If the _____ (Koran) is right, then _____ is a liar.
2. _____ is a false prophet.
3. The ____ are descendants of Ishmael.
4. Islam denies that ____ died on the cross.
5. ____ was the name of the moon-god that preceded ____ Arabian people.
6. The Quran states that ____ are superior to ____ because women are less intelligent.
7. The word, "Islam" is Arabic meaning _____ (not peace as many claim).
8. This false religion teaches and promotes ____ and ____.
9. Either the ____ or the ____ (Koran) is wrong, both cannot be ____.
10. ____ teachings are all ____ and true.

TRUE OR FALSE

1. ____ Muhammad was never married.
2. ____ The Quran teaches that Jesus is God's only begotten Son.
3. ____ Muslims do not follow the one true God in heaven (Isa. 45:5).
4. ____ The Quran teaches that a man can have only one wife.
5. ____ The Quran is an inspired revelation from Jehovah God.

FIVE SIMPLE QUESTIONS

1. What scripture in our study teaches that God's word is truth?
2. By what name is the ancient city of Mecca now called?
3. What does the Quran teach concerning the Godhead?
4. Islam has approximately how many followers?
5. What scriptures in our study tell us to not add to God's word?

26

Plain Bible Talk

ABOUT HEAVEN

PURPOSE
To learn about our eternal heavenly home.

GOAL
To learn from the Bible what heaven will be like.

CHALLENGING THOUGHT
One will not accidentally go to heaven!

KEY WORDS

home	eternity	better
rest	praise	mansion
recognize	place	God

CHOICES BEFORE US
One will either prepare to go to heaven or be in hell forever.

THREE GREAT TRUTHS
There are no changes after death.
Heaven is a real place for prepared people.
God, Jesus, and all the good people of all time will be in heaven.

SCRIPTURES TO BE READ AND STUDIED

John 14:1–3; 3:13	Hebrews 11:10, 16; 12:22–23
1 Peter 1:4	Matthew 6:9; 25:31–34
Philippians 3:20	1 Thessalonians 1:10
2 Timothy 4:6–8	1 Thessalonians 4:16–17

PRAYER FOR TODAY
Dear God, we thank Thee for heaven, our eternal home.

_____

Heaven Is for Me

The entrance fee for heaven is obedience to the gospel and faithful living for a very short time (Acts 2:37-47; Rev. 2;10; 14:13). Surely, no one thinks God is asking too much! When I ponder all the beautiful and endearing things—rainbows, sunsets, babies, grandchildren—they all fade in comparison to heaven. This old world has a vile, foul, and contemptible "smell," but heaven has the fragrance of holiness. Heaven is a real place that has been prepared by Jesus; it is where God lives! Termites cannot destroy it, fire cannot burn it, floods cannot wash it away, and thieves cannot break in. All the good people of all time will be there. Heaven is worth it all! Yes, heaven is for me!

I Really Want to Go There

Heaven is the glory that is to be revealed (1 Pet. 5:1). Only a "fool" would reject what God has prepared for the redeemed. When this old world explodes and belches up the dead, the giant redwood trees snap like toothpicks, the Grand Canyon closes its mouth, the Rocky Mountains are flattened, the islands sink, and Jesus comes in glory, we will then understand the seriousness of dying in the Lord! Yes, I intend to make the journey with Jesus and all His holy angels to my eternal home that is called heaven!

Why I Want to Go to Heaven

1. *Because the choice is heaven or hell.* No other option is available. Hell is a vile, filthy, miserable, painful, dark, and damnable place (Matthew 8:12; 25:46). Kind of narrows the choice down, does it not?

2. *Because God, Jesus, and the Holy Spirit will be there.* The thought of being forever with holiness and deity is appealing to me. Read John 14:1–6.

3. *Because there will be no more suffering and worrying!* No more watching our loved ones suffer, decay, and die. Read Philippians 3:20–21.

4. *Because heaven is a real and beautiful place.* It is not a room, cabin, or even a fine house. It is an estate or mansion (1 Pet. 1:3–5; John 14:1–3).

5. *Because my heart and treasure are there.* This earth is not my home. I am just traveling through. I am only a pilgrim and my journey is short (Heb. 9:27; 1 Pet. 1:1). Without proper investment, there will be no interest in heaven (Matt. 6:19–21).

6. *Because all the faithful of all time will be there!* What a fellowship! What a reunion! What rejoicing! Just imagine: Moses, Mary, Abraham, Paul, and every other faithful child of God will be there. Imagine seeing our brethren and family members again and having immortal bodies that are whole, pure, and complete! Imagine seeing all the babies that have crossed those chilly waters! All those precious little souls that were murdered under the guise of that weasel word, "abortion." Just think, I will have an eternity to talk to Adam, Moses, Martha, and all others I have so long admired. Do not ever think that they will not be excited to see us, too; they will be! There will be recognition in heaven (2 Sam. 12:23; Matt. 17:1–8; Rev. 6:9–11). Heaven holds all to me!

7. *Because my name is enrolled there!* Read Philippians 4:3; 3:20; and Hebrews 12:23. I can hardly wait to hear Jesus call my name!

8. *Because my salvation will be fully finalized!* Read Revelation 2:10 and 2 Timothy 4:6–8.

9. *Because heaven will no longer be just a hope but a reality!* Read I Corinthians 15:19 and Titus 3:7.

10. *Because heaven is a better place* (Phil. 1:23). There will be no honkytonks, dance halls, dens of sin, clinics to murder babies, hospitals, nursing homes, pain, suffering, death, decay, sin, divorce, abused children, or widows and orphans. What a place! What beauty! What happiness and bliss! That is the better country for which I yearn!

Closing Thought

Please note that I did not use Revelation 21–22 as a text to describe heaven. I do not believe those two chapters were written to describe that wonderful place. They describe the church after the onslaught of Rome (Rev. 21:2, 9–10). John saw the church coming down out of heaven into a new environment and away from Rome's persecution. In these two chapters, the word *city* is used twelve times, and each time it refers to 21:2, 9–10, the church! One might use the descriptive terms, but not in context, to talk about heaven, and do no "harm" to the scriptures, but let's be good and honest Bible students. I do not doubt that heaven will be without pain and sorrow, but remember that the context in Revelation 21–22 is the beautiful church away from Rome's persecution.

QUESTIONS

1. One will not accidentally go to _____.
2. _____ is a real place that has been _____ by Jesus, and it is where _____ lives.
3. _____ cannot destroy it, _____ cannot burn it, _____ cannot wash it away, and _____ cannot break in.
4. _____ is a vile, filthy, _____, painful, dark and _____ place (Matt. 8:12, 25:46).
5. In heaven, _____, _____, and the Holy Spirit will be there.
6. Heaven is a _____ place for _____ people.
7. We are only _____ and our journey is _____ (Heb. 9:27; 1 Pet. 1:1).
8. In heaven, there will be no more _____ and worrying.
9. Without proper _____, there will be no _____ in heaven (Matt. 6:19–21).
10. Heaven is a _____ place (Phil. 1:23).

TRUE OR FALSE

1. ____ In context, Revelation 21–22 is describing the church after the Roman persecution.
2. ____ There is no such thing as recognition in heaven.

3. ____ Heaven is always called a small cabin or room.
4. ____ Paul said that it was better to stay here on earth rather than go to be with the Lord.
5. ____ According to 1 Thessalonians 4:13–17, Jesus is coming back and set His feet on this earth.

FIVE SIMPLE QUESTIONS

1. What scriptures tell us that Jesus has prepared a place for the redeemed?
2. What verse tells us that David could go and see his child who had died?
3. What verses in the book of Revelation call the church "the bride of the Lamb"?
4. What verse says it is better to be with Christ?
5. What verse teaches us that it is necessary to be faithful unto death in order to receive the crown?

27

Plain Bible Talk

ABOUT HELL

PURPOSE
To learn more about that terrible and awful place called hell.

GOAL
To learn from the Bible what that place of torment will be like.

CHALLENGING THOUGHT
There is no such thing as getting out of hell; it is forever!

KEY WORDS

forever	darkness	pain
suffering	worm	gnashing of teeth
torment	fire	

CHOICES BEFORE US
Either heaven or hell will be our eternal abode.

THREE GREAT TRUTHS
There is a real place called hell.
All the bad people of all time will be there.
Hell will be full of folks who intended to do better—
    tomorrow!

SCRIPTURES TO BE READ AND STUDIED

Luke 16:19–31	Matthew 8:12; 25:30, 46
Mark 9:48	2 Thessalonians 1:7–9

Hell Is Not for Me

Hell is so awful that prayers are offered by inhabitants to try to prevent others from coming. Hell was prepared for the devil and his angels, and all who reject the ways of God will go there (Matt. 25:31–46). Hell is described as darkness, fire, brimstone, gnashing of teeth (intense suffering), where their worm dieth not, and punishment. Hell is not for me!

Advice from the Place of Torment

From Luke 16:19–31 comes advice to all who are still on this side of death. It would serve us well to heed this advice. The cries from hell are telling us:

1. Be concerned about the way you live, dress, talk, and act. Life on earth is short!
2. Use everything you have in service to God. (This admonition is also for young people!)
3. Be concerned enough about others to tell them about this place! We are now in flames of fire!
4. Do not be deceived by material wealth. Your soul, family, and others are more important.
5. Prepare now. Don't waste another minute. The Bible was true after all!
6. Hell is forever and forever! You don't want any part of it. God is not here.
7. The memory of knowing that you wasted opportunities to obey God will be torment in itself.
8. Pain, suffering, and indescribable torment never cease in this place. Don't come here!
9. Prayers are constantly being offered that you do not come to this horrible place.

10. Hell is a truth learned too late, and we beg every day for our torment to end!

11. Don't go to sleep tonight without making things right with God. Hell is no joke!

12. There are no changes after death. God really means what He says!

Why I Do Not Want to Go to Hell

1. *Because I will be conscious in that awful place and all the damned of all time will be there!* (Luke 16:22–23). There is no sleep or rest in that terrible place. If the weak-kneed members of the church really believed hell is as bad as the Bible teaches, they would become faithful today! If one dies unprepared, he is not better off, even though he might be suffering beyond measure in this life. The only time many utter the word *hell* is to use it wrongly! There is no politically correct way to talk about hell! There is no weasel word for hell! I do not want to go to the devil's hell!

2. *Because I will know others in that awful place!* (Luke 16:23–24). If I go to hell, I will be side by side with Hitler, Domitian, rapists, murderers, baby killers, abusers of children—all the evil I try to stay away from in this life! And yes, those in hell will know others in hell (2 Sam. 12:23; Matt. 17:1–7; Rev. 6:9–11). Hell's inhabitants will be with the worst people who ever lived on earth! I don't want to be in that place!

3. *Because I will have a memory of all my wasted opportunities to do good and to be in heaven!* (Luke 16:25, 27–28). In hell, no one will ever encourage me to repent, be baptized, or live right! No more sermons, Bible classes, preachers, or elders! All those who made efforts to change the work and worship of the Lord's church will remember. All atheists will remember their blasphemous words against God. Church members who never gave as they were prospered, never taught anyone, never attended faithfully, never considered the sacredness of the blood-stained cross, never really participated in the singing, and never made a habit of praying will remember. I don't want any part of that place!

4. *Because the lost in torment are now praying that I don't go there!* (Luke 16:27–28). It must be a terrible and agonizing place of suffering. The lost are really and truly lost forever. I don't want to be among those who are now praying in hell, because God does not hear them.

5. *Because I will know my final and eternal destiny is hell!* (Luke 16:22–23). I will not have to be concerned about Jesus' second coming. The books will be opened, and I will stand before the great white throne and will not have a choice in the matter. God will not suggest that I do either! I will forever be lost. I don't want to hear my Jesus say, "Depart!"

6. *Because many in hell depended on the "finer" things on earth!* (Luke 16:19). Many never learned that people—not things—are important. In hell no one will have the purple robes or the ivory beds! Everything is left behind! "Golden calves" (materialism) will send multitudes to hell (Mark 4:19). I do not desire to go to that awful place!

7. *Because of the flames of torment!* (Luke 16:23). No babies there, no relief, and no changes once you get there. Imagine the last words from your little girl: "You cannot go with me; you cannot be my daddy anymore." What agony! Hell is not for me!

8. *Because of the never-ending begging in hell!* (Luke 16:24). Begging for medication, water, relief, another invitation song, one more sermon, one more opportunity, or one hour's rest. I do not want any part of that awful place!

9. *Because God is not in hell!* (Luke 16:24, 27). This is the only place where God is not. The multitudes who have claimed they did not need God will have their wish! God will not hear their prayers or see their pain and suffering. Those who think they do not need God should quit eating, breathing, and living because all this comes from God! Hell is not for me!

10. *Because hell is not heaven!* (Luke 16:25–26). Hell is a place of tears, pain, agony, sin, hurt, screams, torment, anger, and bitterness. None of these things will enter heaven. No wonder the place of torment is the "second death." I don't want to go to hell!

QUESTIONS

1. There is no such thing as getting out of _____, it is _____!
2. _____ is full of folks who intended to do _____—tomorrow!
3. There are no _____ after death and _____ really means what He says.
4. If _____ of the church really believed this place was as bad as the _____ teaches, they would become _____ today.
5. The _____ of knowing that you wasted _____ to obey God is _____ in itself.
6. All _____ will remember their blasphemous words against God.
7. I don't want to hear my Jesus say, "_____!"
8. Many never learn that it is _____, and not _____ that are important.
9. _____ ("golden calves") will send many to _____.
10. _____, _____ and indescribable _____ never cease in this place.

TRUE OR FALSE

1. ____ Hell was prepared only for the devil and not his angels.
2. ____ No one ever prays in that awful place.
3. ____ Gnashing of teeth means intense pain.
4. ____ We will recognize others in hell.
5. ____ Hell is a temporary place of punishment.

FIVE SIMPLE QUESTIONS

1. What verses in Luke 16 teach that folks will be conscious in the place of torment?
2. What verses in Luke 16 teach that there is praying in the place of torment?
3. What verse in Luke 16 teaches that there are flames of torment in this awful place?
4. What verse in Luke 16 teaches that there is begging in the place of torment?
5. What verses in Luke 16 teach that there is recognition in the place of torment?

28

Plain Bible Talk

ABOUT BEATITUDES

PURPOSE
To learn more about the beatitudes found in Matthew and Revelation.

GOAL
To apply the lessons learned from the beatitudes to our daily lives.

CHALLENGING THOUGHT
Practicing the beatitudes will change our lives forever.

KEY WORDS

beatitudes	happy	blessed
heart	thinking	affection
salvation		

CHOICES BEFORE US
Either we will learn to be happy and content or to be self-serving and miserable.

THREE GREAT TRUTHS
The beatitudes will change one's heart.
The beatitudes will make one right with God.
The beatitudes will cause one to consider the lost souls of mankind.

SCRIPTURES TO BE READ AND STUDIED
Matthew 5:1–11   Revelation 16:15; 19:9
Revelation 1:3; 14:13   Revelation 20:6; 22:7; 22:14.

PRAYER FOR TODAY
Dear God, give me a good heart and an attitude that is right.

What Is a Beatitude?

The word *beatitude* means blessed or happy and is used for the collection of sayings Jesus used to introduce His sermon on the mount. A beatitude has to do with the heart and attitude of an individual. Jesus stated these beatitudes for His disciples to practice in order to develop the spiritual character needed to do His work. By practicing these beatitudes, we too will develop the proper heart and attitude. We can then receive His blessings, do His work, and know how to deal with circumstances in life, including persecution.

The Beatitudes of Matthew 5:1–11

Blessed are:

- The poor in spirit (those who submit to God and His will).
- They that mourn (those who experience heartache because of sin).
- The meek (those lacking arrogance).
- They which do hunger and thirst after righteousness (have a driving desire to know and do right).
- The merciful (those who forgive their fellowman).
- The pure in heart (those who have no evil intentions or desires).
- The peacemakers (those who promote unity and peace based on truth and righteousness).
- They which are persecuted for righteousness' sake (those who are not discouraged by those who are offended by good and righteousness acts).
- Ye, when men shall revile and persecute you (those who are abused and mistreated by evil men).

Matthew 5 tells us what takes place when a person practices these beatitudes. He will live right (v. 20), have the right kind of heart (v. 22), worship right (v. 23), have the right attitude (v. 25), think right (v. 27), talk right (v. 34), have the right influence (v. 38), and love right (vv. 43–48).

The Seven Beatitudes of the Book of Revelation

The seven beatitudes found in the book of Revelation deal with Scripture's great themes: Bible, death, faithfulness, church, heaven and hell, God, and baptism. Note these beatitudes:

1. 1:3. *"Blessed are those who wait on God."* John is telling us to wait on God for all our answers. The Bible can and must be understood and it has the right answer on every subject (Ps. 119:128). We need to reintroduce ourselves to the Bible! Spiritual ignorance will cause us to be just another denomination. Read Hosea 4:1, 6; Isaiah 5:13; 2 Timothy 2:15; Matthew 22:29; Jeremiah 22:29.

2. 14:13. *"Blessed are those who die in the Lord."* The only thing that really matters is to die in the Lord! In order to do so, one must live in the Lord. Many members of the church are dying spiritually. This can be prevented by knowing the Bible, loving the one true New Testament church, and knowing that God is in control.

3. 16:15. *"Blessed are those who are faithful."* (See also 2:10.) Christians and congregations must guard their identity. The Christian life is worth living and the church is worth fighting for. Our neighbors must know and see a difference between us and the religious world! Make a stand for the right and a stand against the wrong. It matters how we talk, dress, and act.

4. 19:9. *"Blessed are those who love the church."* Also read the first eight verses. Blessed are those who are members of the church, the beautiful bride of Christ. If the church loses its purpose, it loses everything! There is but one church—bride (Matt. 16:18; Acts 2:37–47; Rom. 16:16; Eph. 1:22–23, 4:4). The church must realize its purpose, work, importance, and glory. It must rebuke and expose false teachers. It must know the Bible. The world must see these things.

5. 20:6. *"Blessed are those who avoid hell and enter heaven."* The faithful will not face the second death (hell) but will enjoy the beauties of heaven. Again, there is no polite way to talk about hell. It is a terrible, awful, agonizing pit! Blessed is the one who avoids that eternal place of flames.

6. 22:7. *"Blessed are those who are prepared for God's judgment."* He who believes, obeys, respects, defends, accepts, practices, and teaches the Bible is blessed. The Bible will judge us in the last day (John 12:48). Many do not fear God! (Rom. 3:18). They will be surprised and shocked on judgment day when they find out God meant what He said! God will not—He cannot!—change His law on judgment day for anyone! He will not let sin "slide."

7. 22:14. *"Blessed are those who are baptized and can approach God."* Why is the baptized person blessed? (22:14; 1:5; Acts 22:16). Because he is saved, added to the church, and has the right to approach God in worship! What a blessing! Scripturally baptized people are indeed blessed.

QUESTIONS

1. The _____ will cause one to consider the _____ souls of mankind.

2. A beatitude has to do with the _____ and _____ of an individual.

3. Blessed are the _____ in spirit (those who submit to God and His will).

4. The seven beatitudes in the book of Revelation deal with the themes of_____, _____, _____, _____, _____ and _____, _____ and _____.

5. The_____ can and must be understood and it has the _____ answer on every _____.

6. The only thing that really matters is to _____ in the Lord!

7. Blessed are those who are _____ of the church (the beautiful _____ of Christ).

8. For the one who _____, _____, _____, _____,
_____, _____ and _____ the Bible, he is blessed.
9. Scripturally _____ people are indeed blessed.
10. The church must realize its _____, work, importance, and
glory.

TRUE OR FALSE

1. ____ The word *beatitude* means sorry or regretful.
2. ____ Peacemakers promote peace and unity that are based on truth
and righteousness.
3. ____ Spiritual ignorance will cause us to be more Christ like.
4. ____ One can die in the Lord even though he did not live in the Lord.
5. ____ The Christian life is worth living and the church is worth fighting for.

FIVE SIMPLE QUESTIONS

1. What verse in the book of Revelation says those who die in the Lord
are blessed?
2. What verse plainly states that baptism washes away sins?
3. Where is the verse that teaches the Bible will judge us in the last
day?
4. What verse says, "The churches of Christ salute you"?
5. What verse teaches that the meek will be blessed?

29

Plain Bible Talk

ABOUT GAMBLING

PURPOSE
To learn more about the evils and sin of gambling.

GOAL
To expose the harm that gambling brings upon our society and to avoid it.

CHALLENGING THOUGHT
Gambling violates every right precept found in the Bible.

KEY WORDS

gamble	chance	sin
risk	lottery	crime
covetous	bet	immoral

CHOICES BEFORE US
Either the Bible is right or gambling is good and right.

THREE GREAT TRUTHS
Gambling breeds dishonesty.
Gambling is a destroyer of homes.
Gambling will never make for a better society.

SCRIPTURES TO BE READ AND STUDIED

2 Samuel 24:24	Ecclesiastes 5:10
Matthew 7:12	1 Thessalonians 5:22
Ephesians 4:28	Colossians 3:5
Romans 12:17	1 Corinthians 15:33
Revelation 18:4	

PRAYER FOR TODAY
Dear God, help me always to be a good example to others.

Gambling Defined

To gamble is "to play a game for money or other stakes, to bet on an uncertain outcome, to risk by gambling, a wager, the playing of a game of chance for stakes." Gambling is the risk of putting up one's money or possessions in expectation (or hope) of gaining what others possess without just payment. Gambling's definition alone condemns its practice!

The Wrongs of Gambling

1. Gambling causes hard feelings, resentment, and strife. Gambling for a penny or a million dollars is sin. It is the same as stealing one penny or a million dollars or telling a big whopper of a lie or a little white lie. Both are wrong. The amount has nothing to do with it. There are some twenty million Americans with serious gambling problems. Gambling is not harmless fun! It divides families and friends.

2. Making gambling legal does not make it right; it is still sin. Legalizing whiskey, murder (abortion), divorce, homosexuality, or nudist colonies does not make them right. God's law will forever stand (Ps. 119:89). There is no right way to do a wrong thing!

3. Regardless of who condones, participates in, or encourages it, gambling is still sin. Just because some churches, schools, clubs, states, and boys' and girls' ball teams sponsor cake walks and bingo games, sell chances, and promote raffles or fish ponds at fall carnivals, that does not make gambling right!

4. It does not matter whether it is chances sold by children for a "worthwhile" cause or a slot machine in Vegas grabbing granny's quarters, gambling is still gambling. Casino is spelled with sin—ca-SIN-o. Location does not change sin to right!

5. Here are some ways folks gamble:
   - Betting on races: horses, frogs, and dogs.
   - Playing cards, throwing dice, pulling slot machines levers.

- Betting on sports—yes, even dog and rooster fights, as well as human sporting events
- Buying chances on a TV, a gun, or a bull.
- Baseball throws, ring tosses, pitching pennies, odd man out, or pulling coke bottles to see which one was made the farthest away.

  Gambling is sin!

6. Gambling is based on the principle of something for nothing. It truly violates every right precept!

7. Gambling is still wrong even if two or more people agree to do it. What if the same two or more agreed to commit adultery or watch pornography? If I agreed with another to steal his car for insurance money, would we still be sinning? Of course we would!

8. Gambling is wrong even if the money goes for a good cause. Is a drug dealer justified in his business if he gives the money to the Lord? There is no such thing as "necessary sin" (Prov. 28:21). Regardless of the reason, gambling is always wrong.

9. Gambling is sin even if the stakes are small. Can one cuss just a little? Practice a little homosexuality? Engage in a little fornication? Take a little dope? Then how can anyone justify penny-ante gambling?

10. Gambling is sin even though the Bible does not mention the word *gamble.* Neither are the words *beer* and *cocaine* mentioned in the Bible! The principle of gambling is condemned by the Bible. The Bible does not specifically condemn every sinful action. For example, the Bible does not say, "Thou shalt not worship Elvis Presley," but it is wrong to do so! (Rev. 22:9). Gambling is covetousness (Col. 3:5); it violates the Golden Rule (Matt. 7:12); it is robbery by consent (Eph. 4:28); it does not follow the example of Jesus (1 Pet. 2:21); it is dishonest; it destroys (Rom. 12:17); it does not express love for others (Matt. 22:29–39); and it absolutely devastates one's influence (1 Pet. 2:12). Some even rob piggy banks to gamble.

11. Gambling always produces harm and destruction. It never brings about "betterment." It promotes prostitution. Gambling (lotteries) will not solve our educational financial problems! Some states are

now realizing that gambling creates more problems than it solves.

12. Gambling is poor stewardship of God's blessings, the one sure bet. You gamble; you lose. And so do others!

Some Common Objections Answered

1. *Farming is a gamble.* No, it is providing for others by hard and honest work (1 Tim. 5:8).

2. *The Bible does not say, "Do not gamble."* Neither does it say, "Thou shalt not rob banks."

3. *A business is a gamble.* No! A businessman must invest in order to produce. He produces or invests in a product and makes it available to others (Acts 16:14).

4. *Gambling is fun and I like it.* Some think drinking beer and going naked is fun (Heb. 11:25).

5. *Buying stock is a gamble.* No, it is joint ownership. Benefits are derived from such.

6. *Buying insurance is a gamble.* No, it aids in an emergency or need. Both the purchaser and provider benefit in the financial investment. Insurance is an investment in exchange for protection.

7. *Selecting another apostle was a gamble.* No. This argument demonstrates the silliness of trying to defend gambling. No chance was involved! Read Numbers 26:55; 1 Chronicles 24:5; Proverbs 16:33; and Acts 1:26. No money or wager was engaged. God was in control; there was no chance involved whatsoever!

8. *Playing the stock market is a gamble.* No, this is a means of buying and selling. It is like a lemonade stand or a car dealership.

9. *Winning door prizes is a gamble.* No, the one who received a free ticket did not make a purchase in order to gamble. The store uses this for advertising (or courtesy), like a TV or radio ad.

10. *Everyday living is a gamble.* No, God is in control (Isa. 40:22). Life is no gamble!

QUESTIONS

1. Gambling is a _____ of homes.
2. Gambling for a _____ or a _____ dollars is sin.
3. _____ is spelled with *sin*.
4. Gambling is sin even if _____ or more _____ to do it.
5. The Bible does specifically condemn every _____ action.
6. Gambling always produces _____ and destruction.
7. Gambling is _____ stewardship of _____ blessings.
8. Gambling is sin even if a person gambles with a "_____ money."
9. There are some _____ million American people with serious _____ problems.
10. There is no _____ way to do a _____ thing.

TRUE OR FALSE

1. ____ Gambling breeds dishonesty.
2. ____ It is not wrong to gamble, cuss, steal, or lie just a little.
3. ____ Gambling is not wrong if it is for a good cause.
4. ____ Since the Bible does not say, "Thou shalt not pour carbolic acid into a baby's eye," it is right to do so.
5. ____ Farming is a gamble.

FIVE SIMPLE QUESTIONS

1. What is the meaning of the word *gamble?*
2. What scripture in Psalms says God's Word is forever settled in heaven?
3. Should a child sell chances on an item to raise money for his school? Defend your answer.
4. What scripture says covetousness is idolatry?
5. What is the one sure bet?

30

Plain Bible Talk

ABOUT SEEKING
A NEW WAY

PURPOSE
To learn that God meant what He said concerning all matters.

GOAL
To study an Old Testament example that will help the church fulfill its purpose.

CHALLENGING THOUGHT
The reason so many are trying to change the church is because of a lack of fear and respect for God and His Word (Rom. 3:18).

KEY WORDS

authority	fear	respect
change	tamper	consequences
example	ark	box

CHOICES BEFORE US
Either we will believe that God really meant what He said and obey it, or we will change what God has said and try new ways.

THREE GREAT TRUTHS
God will not let sin slide.
God will not allow any man to change His Word.
Time does not nullify God's commands.

SCRIPTURES TO BE READ AND STUDIED

Romans 15:4	Colossians 3:17
Exodus 25:10–22	Hebrews 9:4
2 Samuel 6:1–7	1 Chronicles 15:2, 12–13
Job 8:8	

PRAYER FOR TODAY

Dear God, help us to learn and apply truths from times of old.

Introduction

1. Three different arks are mentioned in the Bible: Noah's huge boat (Gen. 6), baby Moses' ark of bulrushes (Exod. 2), and God's ark of the covenant (Exod. 25). The latter is our subject matter. It was a box (4' x 2' x 2') made of acacia (shittim) wood and overlaid with gold. It contained the golden pot of manna (Exod. 16:33), Aaron's rod that budded (Num. 17:10), and the tables of law (Exod. 25:16; Deut. 10:2). The ark symbolized God's presence. It was highly respected and cherished.

2. God gave plain and specific instruction concerning how the ark was to be carried and by whom (Exod. 25:12–15; Num. 4:1–16; Deut. 31:9, 25–26; Josh. 3:1–6).

3. First Samuel 4–6 is an account of Israel in battle with the Philistines. Because of a lack of trust in God, Israel was losing. They called for the ark. The Philistines had captured it and set it before Dagon, their god. They had held it for seven months. Dagon was in the form of a man from the waist up and of a fish from the waist down. By the next morning, Dagon had fallen before the ark. They set their god back in its place, but by the following morning it had fallen again, and its head and hands had broken off. The Philistines were then smitten with tumors and eventually called for their priests to get rid of the ark. The priests built a new cart, loaded the ark on it, and pulled it away with two cows.

4. Eventually, David wanted to bring the ark "back home" (2 Sam. 6:1–5). Even though God had given instructions for transporting

the ark four hundred years earlier, David used the Philistine's method instead of God's. He built a new cart and pulled it with two cows. Calamity engulfed Israel. God was angry with Uzzah for touching the ark, even though Uzzah meant well (2 Sam. 6:7). God was angry with Israel. She was doing the right thing in the wrong way! Nothing was going well for Israel, and David said it was because they were not following God's instructions on transporting the ark (1 Chron. 15:2, 12–13). When they obeyed this command, blessings followed.

What Do We Learn from This? (Rom. 15:4)

1. Religious denominations do not establish the standard of truth. We must have authority for all we do (Col. 3:17). Just let a religious group come up with a new idea and presto, the church follows! Can you imagine Noah saying, "If you get on the ark, I will give you a free elephant!" We must use the gospel and not gimmicks to convert others. There is not a new way!

2. Following man's way is an eternal tragedy (Exod. 23:2; Jer. 10:23). Like Nadab and Abihu (Lev. 10:1–2) and Moses (Deut. 1:37), the Jews were doing the right thing in the wrong way. Read Proverbs 14:12 and Jeremiah 6:16; 18:15. The ark should never have been on the cart to start with!

3. Just being sincere is not enough (Josh. 24:14; 2 Cor. 2:17). No one was more sincere than the young prophet (1 Kings 13:9, 11, 18, 24), but he was wrong. Paul was sincere while persecuting the church (Acts 23:1; 26:9), but he was wrong. Truth must be involved! Uzzah was sincere!

4. We must indoctrinate the next generation with the pure gospel (Judg. 2:10; 2 Tim. 2:2). They must know about the one church, its founder, its worship, and its purpose. They must hear strong sermons on hell, adultery, immorality, immodesty, and sin in general.

5. It does make a difference how we do things (1 Chron. 15:2, 12, 13). We must do what God commands the way He said to do it. Ask Uzzah, Nadab and Abihu, Moses, the young prophet, the Jews who

wandered in the wilderness, and many other characters of the Bible if it matters how we do things! Does it matter what medicine a person takes, what direction he travels, or what doctor he uses? It also matters how we worship!

6. Public repentance and a return to God's ways are needed (Jer. 6:16; Matt. 18:15–17; Luke 17:3–4). We must make our stand upon truth (Eph. 6:13). Challenge the church changers to repent! Make your stand and don't be moved (1 Cor. 15:58).

7. Time does not change or nullify God's law (Ps. 119:89; Matt. 24:35). The Bible reads the same now as it did in AD 50. It will read the same when we stand before God in judgment. Some four hundred years went by between God's command not to touch the ark and Uzzah's touching it! We worship the same way today as Christians did in Acts 2 (Rev. 22:18–19). Which of the qualifications could the Jews change concerning being a priest? (Num. 4:1–3). Which qualification can we change concerning an elder? (1 Tim. 3:1–7; Tit. 1:1–16). Which requirement can we change concerning becoming a Christian? The Lord's supper? Singing? Answer: None!

8. Tragedy is the fruit of trying to be like everybody else (1 Sam. 8:4–9; Matt. 15:12–14). The Israelites thought the Philistines had a great idea but never considered whether or not it was authorized by God. This causes the church to lose its purpose and identity. We become just another religion.

9. Sin should cause us to fear God and respect His commandments (2 Sam. 6:6–11). We must learn from our mistakes and do better. We are often influenced by the wrong people. Always ask, "Is this authorized by God?" We must watch whom we fellowship (Eph. 5:11).

10. Disaster will always be the result of disobeying God (1 Chron. 15:2; 12–13). We cannot hide or run from God. Until Israel corrected the way they carried the ark, disaster followed them. Do I really believe it mattered how they carried that box (ark)? Yes! And so should you (Rom. 15:4).

Questions

1. _____ does not nullify God's commands.
2. The ark (Ex. 25) was made of _____ (shittim) wood and was overlaid with _____.
3. The ark symbolized _____ presence and was highly _____.
4. _____ was the god of the Philistines.
5. _____ touched the ark and died.
5. We must use the _____ and not _____ to convert others.
6. Following _____ way is an eternal _____.
7. The _____ thought the _____ had a great idea, but never considered if it was _____ by God.
8. _____ will always be the result of _____ God.
9. We must indoctrinate the next _____ with the pure _____.
10. Dagon was in the form of a _____ from the waist up and a _____ from the waist down.

True or False

1. ____ The ark contained Moses' garments and Aaron's spear.
2. ____ God was angry with Uzzah for touching the ark.
3. ____ God commanded the Jews to transport the ark by using two milk cows and a new cart.
4. ____ We must always do what God says in the way He says to do it.
5. ____ There are three different arks mentioned in the Bible.

Five Simple Questions

1. How many years elapsed between God's command not to touch the ark and Uzzah's touching it?
2. How does God react to sincerity without obedience?
3. Why should sin cause us to fear God and respect His commandments?
4. Name the three different arks found in the Bible.
5. What verse in "Scriptures to Be Read and Studied" teaches us to inquire of the former generation?

31

Plain Bible Talk

ABOUT PRAYER

PURPOSE
To learn more about prayer.

GOAL
To learn why, when, where, and how to pray, and then what to ask for.

CHALLENGING THOUGHT
When a Christian prays, he is actually talking to Almighty God!

KEY WORDS

Father	Jesus	name
humble	forgiveness	thanksgiving
hindrance	amiss	

CHOICES BEFORE US
Either one will pray as God directs or he will speak words in vain.

THREE GREAT TRUTHS
Prayer is powerful.
Prayer changes things.
Worry is a prayer to the wrong god.

SCRIPTURES TO BE READ AND STUDIED

Matthew 6:9–15	John 15:7, 16
Hebrews 4:16	1 John 3:22; 5:14
James 4:3; 5:16	1 Thessalonians 5:17
1 Samuel 12:23	Luke 11:1
2 Chronicles 7:14	

PRAYER FOR TODAY

Dear God, please help us to learn how to pray.

Introduction

Not counting those in the book of Psalms, there are some 650 prayers in the Bible, and 450 of those have recorded answers. Prayer is mentioned 25 times in connection with the life of Christ. We need to say something to God every day. Prayer will give our minds a bath. It is sad that some 20 percent of member of the church of Christ never pray. We need to learn how to pray, and then we need to pray!

General Thoughts

1. A lack of praying may be the reason more is not being done to God's honor and glory.
2. Make (and take) time to pray every day. God refuses our requests sometimes because He loves us.
3. A person can teach, sing, or pray false doctrine. We need to learn how to pray.
4. One sins by not praying (1 Sam. 12:23). Pray to forgive and to be forgiven (Matt. 6:14–15).
5. By praying, we find mercy, grace, and help in time of need (Heb. 4:16).
6. God will give exceedingly and abundantly above what we ask or think (Eph. 3:20).
7. One must believe in order to receive (Matt. 21:22).
8. There is a time to pray and a time to work (Josh. 7:10; Exod. 14:15).
9. Boards of education cannot stop children from praying!
10. Only Christians can approach God in prayer and call Him Father.

Why Pray?

1. God has blessed us with this avenue to talk to Him (Heb. 4:16).
2. It is sin not to pray (1 Sam. 12:23).
3. God will bless us for doing so. (Even thought God knows what we need before we ask, He wants to hear from us.)
4. Prayer will accomplish great things. It is powerful; it can reach around the world.
5. We must pray in order to receive (1 John 3:22).

When and Where to Pray?

1. The simple answer is anytime and anywhere (1 Thess. 5:17).
2. Bible characters prayed during the day and night, in the bed, while working, and before eating.
3. If Jesus could pray while on the cross, surely we can pray in our comfortable cars and houses.

How to Pray?

1. To God (Matt. 6:9). It is sin to pray to Jesus; we have no authority to do so.
2. In the name of Christ (John 15:16).
3. According to God's will (1 John 5:14).
4. Not selfishly (James 4:3).
5. Believing you will receive (Matt. 21:22).
6. Without quoting scripture to God and asking for the kingdom to come.

What to Pray For

1. Anything that is good (John 15:7). But prayer is not a shopping list!
2. What we will use wisely.
3. Not frivolous things, but necessities such as daily bread, shelter, and clothing.
4. Forgiveness from God and the ability to forgive others.
5. Gratitude for blessings: Jesus, the church, heaven, and the Bible.
6. The sick, lost, widows, orphans, our country, our president, our children, and the Lord's church.

Must We Be Reverent While Praying?

1. Yes (Matt. 6:9). We are communicating with the one God who made it all!

2. It is a sin to degrade God by approaching Him as a peer: "Pop," "Daddy," "Big Man Upstairs," and "Dad" are too familiar in our culture for addressing God (Matt. 6:9).

3. We have words in our language that are solemn and respectful terms when referring to God—Thee, Thou, Thine. As for me, I will use them when praying (Heb. 12:28). This allows me to elevate God and His name above my wife or pal!

What Are Some Hindrances to Prayer?

1. *Requesting violations of God's natural laws.* Example: A man falling ten stories to the concrete will be hurt regardless of how much he prays on the way down.

2. *Selfishness* (James 4:3).

3. *Contention in the home* (1 Pet. 3:7).

4. *Not forgiving others* (Matt. 6:14–15; Luke 17:3–4).

5. *Unbelief and doubt* (Matt. 21:22; James 1:6).

6. *Failing to do our part* (Josh. 7:10, Exod. 14:15).

7. *Practicing sin* (John 9:31).

8. *Praying to Jesus or Mary* (Matt. 6:9). Why would anyone want to find another way to pray? Could Jesus pray to Himself? Through whom would He pray?

9. *Dishonesty* (Rom. 13:8).

10. *Desire to be seen of men or just to sound good* (Matt. 6:5–8).

QUESTIONS

1. When a Christian prays, he is actually _____ to _____ God.

2. Prayer is mentioned _____ times in connection with the _____ of Christ.

3. Only _____ can approach God in prayer and call him, " _____."

4. God knows what we _____ before we ask.

5. Bible characters prayed during the _____ and _____, while _____, before _____ etc.

6. Don't quote _____ to God, and don't ask for the _____ to come. It has already come (Col. 1:13).

7. It is sin to call God "_____", "_____", "big ____ _____", "_____" etc. (Matt. 6:9).

8. Prayer will give our _____ a bath.

9. God will _____ exceedingly and _____ above what we _____ (Eph. 3:20).

10. _____ is a prayer to the wrong "god."

TRUE OR FALSE

1. ____ We must pray in order to receive.

2. ____ Praying with unbelief and doubt will hinder one's prayer.

3. ____ Prayer must be in the name of Christ.

4. ____ A person sins by not praying.

5. ____ There is ample biblical authority to pray to Mary.

FIVE SIMPLE QUESTIONS

1. When and where can one pray?

2. If one does not pray as God directs, what will result?

3. How can a Christian avoid teaching, singing, or praying false doctrine?

4. There are how many prayers in the Bible? How many recorded answers?

5. What verse in "Scriptures to Be Read and Studied" tells us that the disciples asked Jesus to teach them to pray?

32

Plain Bible Talk

ABOUT HARD QUESTIONS

PURPOSE
To learn what many are calling hard and difficult questions.

GOAL
To study some hard questions and reveal their simple answers.

CHALLENGING THOUGHT
A hard question is simply not wanting to hear God's answer.

KEY WORDS

Bible	if	hard
opinion	versions	inspiration
revelation	simple	difficult

CHOICES BEFORE US
Either the Bible is understandable or God lied to us (Rev. 1:3).

THREE GREAT TRUTHS
One cannot teach what he does not know.
Christians are responsible for knowing the Bible.
Far too many Christians are running from truth.

SCRIPTURES TO BE READ AND STUDIED

Joel 3:14	John 8:32; 17:17; 6:60
2 Corinthians 11:3	2 Timothy 3:15

PRAYER FOR TODAY
Dear God, I pray for wisdom as I apply knowledge to my mind.

Some Simple Observations

1. When God says a thing, that settles it, whether I believe it or not.
2. There are multitudes in the valley of decision, and they desire biblical answers.
3. The Bible is God's inspired book and is His authority for all things (Col. 3:17).
4. The Bible is complete, perfect, and eternal (Jude 3; James 1:25; Matt. 24:35).
5. The Bible is plain and understandable (2 Tim. 3:15; Eph. 3:3–4).
6. The Bible cannot be broken, changed, or altered (John 10:35, Rev. 22:18–19).
7. The Bible is the source of all the right answers (John 12:48; Phil. 3:16; Ps. 119:128).
8. The Bible must be studied, rightly divided, and taught (2 Tim. 2:15; Jer. 22:29).
9. The Bible produces faith and presents the only true pattern for worship and general conduct (Rom. 10:17, Josh. 22:28; 2 Tim. 1:13).
10. Many preachers are too concerned about being politically correct (Gal. 1:10).

Is It Really Hard and Difficult?

A few years ago, I submitted a list of questions to two preachers. Their answers were: "These questions are too hard and difficult," "I am struggling with these questions," and "It would take volumes to answer these questions."

That is unbelievable! The questions could have been answered by a yes or no and a Bible verse. The answers could be written on a postage stamp and have room to spare! The problem with many preachers is that they do not know the Bible and are not preaching enough Bible "to save a gnat" or "fill up a thimble"! Let us see just how "hard and difficult" these questions are to answer (1 Pet. 3:15).

Hard Questions (John 6:60–68)

Jesus said that He was the food (bread, word) and drink (blood) of eternal life (John 6:52–59). His words offended the disciples! (vv. 60–61). This proves that it does not take very much for folks to get offended at the church, the truth, or the preacher. How could this beautiful and simple lesson offend the disciples? It is truly amazing and yet sad. Many decided they would no longer walk with the Master (v. 66), but Peter gives us the right example (vv. 67–68). What was "hard" about the Master's teaching? Nothing!

Answering Ten "Hard" Questions

1. *Do you believe the Bible is God's inspired and complete will that is to be preached to everyone?*
   Answer: Yes (2 Tim. 3:16–17; 4:2). Hard or difficult? No.
2. *Do you believe there is one and only one church for which Jesus shed all His blood to purchase, and that church is the church of Christ?*
   Answer: Yes (Matt. 16:18; Acts 20:28; Rom. 16:16; Eph. 1:22–23; 4:4). A hard question to answer? No.
3. *Do you believe God made everything on earth and in the heavens, and that the teaching of evolution is a doctrine from hell?*
   Answer: Yes (Gen. 1:1). Did it take volumes to answer? No.
4. *Do you believe that Jesus is the Christ, the only begotten Son of God?*
   Answer: Yes (John 3:16). What is difficult about that?
5. *Do you believe there is only one reason to divorce and remarry?*
   Answer: Yes (Matt. 19:1–9). Hard to answer? Not if you believe the Bible.
6. *Do you believe that you can change the name of the church to the "Community Church" with God's approval?*
   Answer: No (Acts 4:12; Rom. 16:16). Hard? No.
7. *Do you believe one can join a denomination and then defend, support, and teach their doctrine, die while a member of that denomination, and be covered by grace, be saved, and enter heaven?*
   Answer: No (Acts 2:38, 47; 2 Tim. 2:10; Heb. 5:8–9; 2 Thess. 1:7–19; 2 John 9–11). Difficult to answer? No.

8. *Do you believe that God allows women to teach a class comprised of men and women, lead the congregation in singing, or preach from the pulpit in a worship service?*

   Answer: No (1 Tim. 2:8–15; 1 Cor. 14:34). Hard? Difficult? No.

9. *Do you believe a person must be baptized for the remission of sins and understand that fact in order to be saved?*

   Answer: Yes (Mark 16:16; Acts 2:38; 1 Pet. 3:21). Would it take volumes to answer that question? No.

10. *Do you believe there are some brethren who are not to be fellowshipped?*

    Answer: Yes (2 John 9–11; Eph. 5:11). Hard, difficult, or volumes to answer? No.

QUESTIONS

1. "A hard question" is simply not wanting to hear _____ answer.
2. When _____ says a thing, that settles it; whether ____ believe it or not.
3. Many preachers are too concerned about being _____ correct.
4. _____ said that He was the _____ (bread, word) and _____ (His blood) of eternal life.
5. Either the _____ is understandable or _____ lied to us.
6. The _____ is the source for all the _____ answers.
7. _____ are responsible to know the Bible.
8. One cannot teach what he does not _____.
9. There are _____ in the valley of decision and they _____ biblical answers.
10. The Bible is _____, _____, and eternal.

TRUE OR FALSE

1. ____ Jesus' disciples became offended when He condemned them to hell.
2. ____ According to 2 Timothy 3:16–17, only a portion of the Bible is inspired.
3. ____ Jesus purchased the one church with all His blood.
4. ____ Jesus taught that God would accept divorce for any reason.
5. ____ According to Genesis 1:1, evolution is a viable option to the earth's existence.

FIVE SIMPLE QUESTIONS

1. Where does God give us the authority to refer to the one church as the "Community Church"?
2. According to Hebrews 5:8–9, how does a man access eternal salvation?
3. What does 2 Timothy 2:8–15 say about a woman teaching and usurping authority over man?
4. What does 1 Peter 3:21 teach about the relationship of baptism and salvation?
5. What does the Bible teach that our relationship to rebellious Christians should be?

33

Plain Bible Talk

ABOUT IMMODESTY

PURPOSE
To learn it is possible to dress immodestly.

GOAL
To allow the Bible to explain why immodesty is a sin.

CHALLENGING THOUGHT
Modesty is not an option; it is a command of God.

KEY WORDS

fashion	trends	sin
appropriate	lust	nakedness
decency	influence	

CHOICES BEFORE US
Either it matters how one dresses or the Bible is a lie.

THREE GREAT TRUTHS
To dress immodestly is a sin.
Immodesty is wrong for men as well as for women.
Worldly fashions and trends are not the standard for the Christian.

SCRIPTURES TO BE READ AND STUDIED

1 Timothy 2:9–10	1 Thessalonians 5:22
Proverbs 7:10	Genesis 3:7; 38:14, 15, 21
Mark 5:15	Matthew 5:27–28
1 Corinthians 4:9	2 Corinthians 6:14–17
1 Peter 4:1–4	

PRAYER FOR TODAY
Dear God, help me to be pure in heart, action, and dress.

General Observations

1. As Christians (new creatures), we can no longer act, look, talk, or dress like the world (2 Cor. 5:17; Rom. 12:2; 1 Pet. 1:4; Col. 3:1–2). Fashions change but modesty does not!

2. The Bible is crystal clear concerning the Christian's attire (1 Tim. 2:9–10).

3. The word *modest* means orderly, well arranged, decent. The word *shamefacedness* means a sense of shame, modesty that would always restrain a good man from an unworthy act. The word *sobriety* means soundness of mind, self-control.

4. Modesty started with Adam and Eve. Even though they were husband and wife, they knew shame concerning nakedness. God is the one who determined that humans be properly clothed (Gen. 3:5–7). He even placed special emphasis on the attire of priests, because they had to climb the stairs to the altar (Exod. 20:26, 42).

5. Nakedness within itself is not always wrong, else one could not bathe.

6. Our dress should distinguish us from the opposite sex. We should not dress with the intent to "show up" the poor, cause lust, or void our good influence. Our dress must conform to God's requirements and not to society and fashions. Customs must conform to the Bible, and not vice-versa.

7. It does matter how one dresses! (2 Sam. 11:1–5; Rom. 14:7).

8. A young lady once said: "I wear a modest bikini!" How can this be?

9. Immodesty is wrong, whether in Alaska or Florida! (Some ladies do not know how to sit!)

10 What is immodesty? (1) Under dressing; (2) over dressing; (3) unisex dressing.

A Common-Sense Test

1. Look in a mirror and be honest. Am I trying to "flaunt my stuff"?

2. Is my clothing decent? Will it cause someone to lust? Is it appropriate? Does Jesus approve?

3. Will my dress bring glory to God? Would the most godly woman or man I know wear this?

4. Will wearing this harm my influence and reputation? Is this the way a Christian should dress?

5. Would the godly women of the Bible have worn this? Men, would Paul and Jesus have worn it?

6. If you could send a portrait of yourself to heaven, how would you dress for the sitting?

7. If I walked down a deserted street at night, would my dress be an asset or a liability?

Answering Objections

If it is sin to dress immodestly—and it is—then we can know the difference in modest and immodest dress. If someone offered you a hundred thousand dollars to dress modestly, you would not have to ask what modest is. You wouldn't ask, "Is this too short, too low, too skimpy, too revealing, or too provocative?" Sports, McDonald's, Sears, and the armed forces have dress codes. Participants and personnel understand and follow them.

Surely God made it plain enough for us to understand and follow His guidelines. Every time one dresses, it is either right or wrong! Take a look at advertising and tell me that dress does not matter! Elders, preachers, and parents had better wake up because souls are at stake.

1. *I can wear what I wish around the house and family.*
   Answer: What did Adam and Eve do?

2. *Regardless of the way I dress, I have pure thoughts.*
   Answer: Nudist colonies use the same defense. One cannot dress immodestly and have a pure mind! What about others?

3. *Surely you do not object to swimming.*
   Answer: Mixed swimming, yes. Why cannot the males swim at a different time from the females? Why do folks think they almost have to completely undress to go swimming? What about the beholder? Remember 2 Samuel 11:1–5 and Matthew 5:28.

4. *Some will desire and lust regardless of how I dress.*

   Answer: It is true that some would lust after a hairy, one-eyed, giant cyclops wearing a full suit of body armor! But the truth is, fewer will lust after a person who is dressed modestly than a person who is scantily clad. When did David lust, before or after he saw the woman bathing?

5. *It is nobody's business how I dress.*

   Answer: You do have a choice in this matter (Josh. 24:15; Matt. 6:24; 7:13–14), but is it the right choice? Read Romans 14:7 and Colossians 3:17.

6. *Shorts, hot pants, miniskirts, halter tops, bikinis, thongs, and no tops are cooler.*

   Answer: The question is, "Are they modest?" Folks do not dress that way while working in the fields. Also, why do people dress that way in cool weather? Have you ever seen a modest bikini? Modest short shorts? A modest thong? A modest topless man or woman? There are no such things! (James 1:13–15).

7. *I want to be in style.*

   Answer: What if it were the style to go topless, bottomless, or even both? God is not in the style business! Most people are going to hell (Matt. 7:13–14). Do you want to do the stylish thing and go with them?

Summary

Men and women must not only dress modestly but also different from one another. Never put another person's mind in the gutter! The inventor of the miniskirt stated that she designed it to make it easier to seduce men without having to undress! God thought we had enough sense to understand His plain teaching on immodesty (1 Tim. 2:9–10). Both to lust and to cause one to lust are sins. Parents, consider God, the beholders, language, clothing, bodily movements, touching, and influence before you allow your daughter to be a cheerleader or do anything that requires public "undress." May we all be pure in dress and thought.

Modesty is for men too. Anyone who displays his belly-button or underwear is guilty of immodesty. It is a sad day when our elders, teachers, and preachers yield to public opinion concerning dress! Can we no longer blush? (Jer. 6:15). If miniskirts, bikinis, two-piece bathing suits, and topless attire are modest, then please tell me what is immodest!

QUESTIONS

1. _____ fashions and trends are not the standard for the _____.
2. *Modest* means _____, _____ _____, _____.
3. *Shamefacedness* means a sense of _____, _____ that would always restrain a _____ man from an unworthy _____.
4. *Sobriety* means _____ of mind, _____ _____.
5. Our dress should distinguish us from the opposite _____.
6. Immodesty is wrong, whether in _____ or _____!
7. Immodesty is under _____, over _____ and uni-sexual _____.
8. The Bible is crystal _____ concerning the _____ attire.
9. _____ is the one who determined that _____ be properly _____.
10. It does matter how one _____.

TRUE OR FALSE

1. ____ Immodesty is wrong for men as well as for women.
2. ____ One can dress immodestly and still have a pure mind.
3. ____ David was guilty of the sin of lust when he saw a woman bathing.
4. ____ Since God said immodesty is a sin, we can know what is modest and immodest.
5. ____ Modesty is not an option. It is a command of God.

FIVE SIMPLE QUESTIONS

1. What scripture in Proverbs talks about the attire of a harlot?
2. What scripture in Exodus explains how priests had to dress?
3. What scripture tells of a man being clothed and in his right mind?
4. What scripture in Jeremiah teaches that some people can no longer blush?
5. What scripture in 1 Corinthians states that Christians have become a spectacle to the world?

34

Plain Bible Talk

ABOUT JOHN 3:16

PURPOSE
To study what is called the "golden text" of the Bible.

GOAL
To study how this scripture is abused and misused.

CHALLENGING THOUGHT
John 3:16 offends just about every denominational person.

KEY WORDS

for	so	the
that	should	not
but	have	

CHOICES BEFORE US
Those of the religious world either will hear and accept the real truth concerning John 3:16 orwill run from what it really teaches and be offended.

THREE GREAT TRUTHS
Truth must be preached.
The whole truth must be preached.
The whole truth must be preached even if it offends people.

SCRIPTURES TO BE READ AND STUDIED
John 3:16; 8:32   John 17:17; 10:24
Mark 6:3   Matthew 23:33
1 Timothy 1:20

PRAYER FOR TODAY
Dear God, please give me the courage to speak Thy whole truth.

Just Preach John 3:16 and Leave Everybody Alone!

When people ask for plain talk concerning passages like John 3:16, they are not willing to accept what they hear! John 3:16 is probably the most familiar and most oft-quoted scripture, and yet the most misused. The cry of the multitudes is, "Why don't you just preach scriptures like John 3:16 and leave other religious people alone?" Or, "If you would just preach John 3:16 you would not offend every denomination!" Folks who make such statements do not realize what they are asking.

Our Master's Plain Talk Offended Many

Folks in Jesus' day asked for plain talk, but they were not willing to accept the answers (John 10:24; 6:60). Even our Master's own family was offended at Him (Mark 6:3). We need plain talk by preachers, not double talk. It is better to say something than almost to say something! God demanded that His spokesman bark (speak) loudly and not be blind, dumb, and lazy (Isa. 56:9–12). Yes, many will reject plain talk (Amos 7:12). Amos called the women cows (4:1); the men, a basket of overripe and stinking fruit (8:1–3); and the whole nation, a bunch of foreigners (9:7). The same people who begged God to send them a prophet told Amos to go back home because they had enough of him in a hurry! Preaching the truth will always offend someone.

Let Us Now Preach John 3:16 and Not Offend Anyone

1. *For God.* I cannot preach that because atheists will be offended! They proclaim loudly that there is no God. If we erase the words "for God" from this passage, nothing else said in the verse really mat-

ters. Read Genesis 1:1; Psalm 14:1; Isaiah 45:5, 12, 18; and Daniel 2:28.

2. *So loved the world.* I cannot preach this because it offends deists. They believe God created it all and then left man to make it on his own. But note that John 3:16 says God loves us. He is concerned and interested in us. Else, why did He send Jesus to die on Calvary's cross? God made the world and set His laws in force. He is in control (Isa. 40:22; Job 37:6). We must cross out "so loved the world" if we do not want to offend others. (Read Romans 5:8.) God is able to deliver! (Dan. 3:17).

3. *That He gave.* I cannot preach that because it would offend premillennialists. They teach that when Jesus comes, He will set up an earthy kingdom. Jesus plainly stated that His kingdom was not of this world (John 17:4, 11; 18:36). Our heavenly Father gave His Son to purchase the church, God's place of salvation (Dan. 2:44; 2 Tim. 2:10; Acts 20:28). Thus we must do away with "that He gave." (Read 1 John 4:9.)

4. *His only begotten Son.* I cannot preach this because it offends all Jews. If the Christ has come—and He has—then Judaism has no right to exist. No adherent of modern Judaism believes Jesus of Nazareth was the Christ. The Jews look for His coming so Judaism will be restored to its Old Testament order. (Read Galatians 3:23–29.) The Old Testament has been taken out of the way (Rom. 7:6; 10:4; Col. 2:14–17). So "His only begotten Son" cannot be proclaimed without offending folks. This phrase also refutes and "offends" modernism. Modernism denies Jesus' miracles, virgin birth, and resurrection! Read Matthew 1:21–22; 16:21; and John 20:30–31. "His only begotten Son" also offends over a billion Muslims! They deny that God can have a Son!

5. *That whosoever.* I cannot preach that because it offends the millions who follow Calvinism. John Calvin believed that God determines at birth whether a person will be saved or lost, and there is nothing the individual can do about it. The Bible says "whosoever,"

and that proclaims salvation for anybody who obeys (Heb. 5:8–9). Just erase "that whosoever." (Read Matthew 28:18–20.)

6. *Believeth.* I cannot preach this because it offends the Universalist who believes everyone will be saved, even unbelievers. (Read Matthew 25:31–46; John 5:28–29; and Matthew 7:13–14). Thus, mark out "believeth."

7. *In Him.* I cannot preach that because it offends every denomination. Denominations teach that anyone who expresses belief in Christ is saved. But one must get into Christ to be saved (2 Tim. 2:10). John 3:16 denies the very thing every denomination teaches: division and having your own standard. One is baptized into Christ (Gal. 3:26–27) and denominations deny that. The "in Him" must be disregarded because that says everyone gets into Christ the same way. (Read John 14:6 and Acts 2:38, 41, 47).

8. *Should not perish, but have everlasting life.* I cannot preach that because it offends materialists. (They teach that physical death ends a person forever.) *Perish* does not mean complete annihilation, but ruin, destruction, or punishment. The soul will exist forever (1 Cor. 15:35–58), so we must exclude "should not perish but have everlasting life." (Read 1 John 3:2.)

What Can I Preach from John 3:16 and Avoid Offending Anyone?

For, so, the, that, should, not, but, have. Just how much sense does this make? None! But if I avoid offending anyone, that is all I have left! Ridiculous, isn't it? Just imagine trying to teach someone the way of God using only those words! Someone asks, "What must I do to be saved?" and you reply, "For, the, that, should, not, but, have."

QUESTIONS

1. John 3:16 offends just about everyone in _____.
2. The _____ truth must be _____ even if it offends people.
3. Folks in _____ day asked for _____ talk, but were not willing to accept the _____.

4. The eight words one can preach from John 3:16 and not offend anyone are _____, ___, _____, _____, _____, _____, ____, _____.
5. We need plain _____ by preachers, and not _____ talk.
6. Preaching the words "for God" offends the _____.
7. Preaching the words "so loved the world" offends those who believe in _____.
8. The materialist believes and teaches that when a person _____, that is the _____ of him forever.
9. What verse in our study teaches that Jesus' own family was offended at Him? _____
10. God demanded that His spokesman _____ (speak) loudly and not be _____, _____ and _____ (Isa. 56:9–12).

True or False
1. ____ Premillennialism teaches that Jesus will set up an earthly kingdom.
2. ____ The true Jew does not believe that Jesus has come.
3. ____ The Universalist teaches nobody will be saved.
4. ____ Calvinism teaches everyone born is lost.
5. ____ John 14:6 teaches there are many ways to go to the Father.

Five Simple Questions
1. What verse states that only a fool denies God?
2. What verse tells us that Jesus purchased the church with His own blood?
3. What three verses in John teaches that the kingdom is not of this world?
4. What verse in 2 Timothy tells us that salvation is in Christ?
5. What verse tells us that the disciples of Jesus accused Him of having a hard saying?

35

Plain Bible Talk

ABOUT PREVENTING CHURCH PROBLEMS

PURPOSE
To learn how to deal with and prevent problems in the church.

GOAL
To study the book of 1 Corinthians and learn the "formula" of problem solving.

CHALLENGING THOUGHT
Problems will find their way into the church; Satan will see to it!

KEY WORDS

truth	beyond	spiritual
carnal	discipline	righteousness
worship	mature	

CHOICES BEFORE US
This congregation will either deal with problems or allow them to take root and destroy the Lord's church in this place like a cancer!

THREE GREAT TRUTHS
Every church will eventually have problems.
How the church deals with problems is what matters.
God has given us the formula on how to deal with them.

SCRIPTURES TO BE READ AND STUDIED
1 Cor. 1:10–13; 4:6   1 Cor. 5:7; 8:13
1 Cor. 10:7; 11:29   1 Cor. 12:13; 16:13

PRAYER FOR TODAY
Dear God, help me be a troubleshooter and not a troublemaker.

Introduction

1. The background for the church of Christ at Corinth is given in Acts 18:1–11.
2. The congregation was established during Paul's second missionary journey, AD 50–54.
3. This letter was written during Paul's third missionary journey, AD 54–58.
4. The problem-ridden congregation wrote Paul for advice on how to correct the problems (1:11; 5:1; 7:1).
5. Corinth, a very wicked and immoral city, was located in lower Greece.
6. The population at this time was around 400,000.
7. The city burned in 146 BC. It was rebuilt by Julius Caesar in AD 46.
8. The most glorious thing to happen to Corinth is found in Acts 18:8.
9. We know from reading 2 Corinthians that the majority involved in these problems repented, but a few remained rebellious toward Paul and the truth.
10. Paul finally told the defiant few that he had reached his patience limits and would straighten them out when he saw them (2 Cor. 13:1–3).

You Mean the Church of Christ Has Problems?

Yes, because human beings make up the church! The church, as God set it up, is perfect, but people are not perfect, and they sometimes do not act as they ought. If you ever find a perfect group of people—and you will not!—then stay away from it because you will make it imperfect!

How Paul Solved Church Problems (1 Corinthians)

- 1:10–13. *Key thought: Unity.* Believe, teach, and stand firmly on truth. The only way to have unity is to base group conduct on truth and right living. Only the Bible provides that formula. Read Amos 3:2.
- 2:6, 13. *Key thought: Inspiration.* Only by God's inspired Word can problems be solved. Never follow man's teaching; follow God's revealed Word. Read Psalm 119:128.
- 3:1–5, 16. *Key thought: Spiritual.* The carnal (fleshy) appetite will exalt men, and that creates problems. The body should be used to God's glory, but when we forget our purpose, we will begin to satisfy the flesh. Maintaining spiritual matters will solve problems. Read 1 Corinthians 10:7.
- 4:6, 9. *Key thought: Do not go beyond.* Do it God's way! Respecting and obeying God's Word will solve all our problems! The world is watching and we Christians can show them the real way to handle any situation or problem. Read Zechariah 8:23.
- 5:13. *Key thought: Discipline.* This will both solve and prevent many problems! It will save the soul of the sinner, keep the church pure, and glorify our heavenly Father. Read 2 Thessalonians 3:6.
- 6:1–5. *Key thought: Wise judgment.* If the church would handle its problems from within and not carry them to the barber shop, beauty salon, or secular courts, the church would truly be a city set on a hill! Repentance, confession, prayer, and forgiveness will work! Read Acts 8:18–24.
- 7:1–40. *Key thought: If the home is right, the church will be also.* If every daddy would love his wife and children and be a spiritual leader, and if every mother would be queen of the home, and parents would "re-take" the home from the children, all would be well. Read Colossians 3:18–21.
- 8:13. *Key thought: Abusing our liberties.* Even though God has granted certain liberties to mature Christians, we are to abstain from those things that might cause a brother to stumble. Restraint goes a long way in solving problems. Read Romans 14:21.
- 9:14. *Key thought: Real Bible preachers.* If we would train and

support more men who respect and preach truth, many common problems would never arise. Read 2 Timothy 4:2.

- 10:14. *Key thought: Flee from idolatry.* Loving God, Christ, and the church more than anything or anybody will solve church problems. Get rid of the golden calves! Read Mark 4:19.

- 11:20–34. *Key thought: Worship is an appointment with God and He is really present.* The focus of every Christian should be on worship, not on self. Read Matthew 26:26–28.

- 12:12–29. *Key thought: Members.* If each baptized believer would fulfill his role in the church, the few problems that would face us could be handled swiftly and efficiently. Work together! Read verse 25.

- 13:1–13. *Key thought: Grow up and love one another.* Acting mature and practicing true biblical love will make all the demons in hell shake! A forty-pound baby is a "pretty," but a forty-year-old baby is a pity! Read 1 John 4:19–21.

- 14:12. *Key thought: Edify.* Our main objective should be building up the church. The church should be a little piece of heaven on earth. Read Ephesians 4:1–16.

- 15:1–4. *Key thought: Gospel.* If the church would focus on the blood-stained cross and teach and defend it, problems would be few and far between. This is truly good news! Read Acts 20:32.

- 16:1–2. *Key thought: Giving.* If God gets our first and best material things, He will have the rest of us! Our hearts, treasures, and efforts will be dedicated to the church. Read Matthew 6:19–33.

QUESTIONS

1. _____ will find their way into the _____, _____ will see to it!

2. The congregation at Corinth was established during _____ second missionary journey.

3. Corinth was located in lower _____.

4. The only way to have unity is to base it on _____ and right _____.

5. Only by _____ word can problems be _____.
6. The church should be a "_____ _____" of heaven on
   _____.
7. In worship, each Christian should focus on _____, and not
   self.
8. If God gets our _____ and _____ materially, He will get the
   _____ of us!
9. Loving _____, _____ and the _____ more than anything
   or _____, will solve church problems.
10. The city of Corinth burned in the year _____ and was re-
    built by _____ _____ in _____.

True or False

1. ____ First Corinthians was written during Paul's first missionary
   journey (AD 48–49).
2. ____ Corinth was a moral city, a good place in which to live.
3. ____ There are "perfect" people who make up the church at certain
   locations.
4. ____ Paul wrote the book of 1 Corinthians.
5. ____ Worship is an appointment with God.

Five Simple Questions

1. What is God's formula for real unity?
2. From what does Paul tell the Christians to flee in chapter 10?
3. When our Christian liberty might cause the weak to stumble, how
   should we handle that liberty?
4. How does the author describe a 40-year-old baby?
5. What verse in the "Scriptures to Be Read and Studied" commands us
   not to go beyond the Scriptures?

36

Plain Bible Talk

ABOUT THE RAPTURE

Purpose
To study the man-made doctrine of the rapture.

Goal
To prove by the Bible that denominational teaching on the rapture is false to the core!

Challenging Thought
Neither the word *rapture* nor its doctrine is found in the Bible.

Key Words

rapture	kingdom	tribulation
left behind	Antichrist	beast
golden age	Satan	earthly
church		

Choices Before Us
A person believes either the Bible concerning Jesus' second coming or the foolish teaching that Jesus will return to set up an earthly throne.

Three Great Truths
Jesus will not set up an earthly throne.
No one will be left behind.
The church, God's spiritual kingdom, has been on earth for almost two thousand years.

Scriptures to Be Read and Studied

John 18:34	Daniel 2:44
Genesis 3:15–16	Matthew 16:16–19
Mark 9:1	Colossians 1:13
Revelation 1:9	John 17:4, 11; 18:36
2 Peter 3:10–13	Acts 2:29–31

Prayer for Today
Dear God, we thank Thee for the kingdom that was established on Pentecost.

The "Left Behind" Doctrine (Rapture)

Almost every denomination believes and teaches premillennialism. (For a more extensive discussion of this subject, read chapter 5 of my book on Revelation.) In summary, the doctrine goes like this: God determined in the year 457 BC or 444 BC—the proponents cannot agree—that within 490 literal years all His promises to the Jews and to the world would be fulfilled. After 483 of these 490 years, all was going as planned until the Jews rejected Christ. God had to think fast, so He devised a plan to give the church as a substitute and pacify the Jews. (These premillennialists actually teach that the church was never in the mind of God.) So God stopped His clock until the Jews would accept Christ and an earthly kingdom.

If that is the case, God never intended the time period from the Pentecost of Acts 2 until now. Some time in the future, God will restart His clock to fulfill the last seven years. This will happen at the rapture, the secret calling away of the saints, both dead and living, including the Holy Spirit. Then many will be "left behind" and the book of Revelation will be literally fulfilled. The first three and one-half years after the rapture, called the tribulation, will be peaceful and things will go on as normal. How will that be possible with so many loved ones gone?

Premillenialists call those last three and a half years the "great tribulation." It will be a horrible time. The Antichrist appears with the mark of the beast. Many Christians are killed soon after their conversion. They will be resurrected at the end of the great tribulation. Moses and Elijah are back on earth but are killed by the Antichrist and "raptured" after three and one-half days.

During this horrible time, Russia invades Israel, world famine occurs, mass murder of believers takes place, nuclear war starts, 200 million Red Chinese kill a million people in the war to take Israel. A worldwide epidemic of malignant sores occurs, all drinking water is destroyed resulting in a "big run" on Coca Cola, hundred-pound hailstones fall, mass killings create a river of blood two hundred miles long—on and on we could go.

All these things are a part of the battle of Armageddon. The Lord's second coming occurs just after these things. The Jews again become the chosen people of God. The Lord begins the thousand-year reign in Judah over an earthly kingdom. The golden age begins. When the thousand years are finished, the devil is loosed for a short time. Then eternity begins with the new earth and new heavens.

This Doctrine Is Patently False

What an imagination! Simply put, this whole ridiculous scheme is designed to reach one goal: for Jesus to set up an earthly kingdom! It is a second-chance doctrine; if you are not in the rapture, don't worry because another opportunity comes after the rapture!

1. Nowhere within the pages of Holy Writ is this foolishness taught (John 18:34).
2. Jesus will not reign on earth (Jer. 22:30; Matt. 1:11; John 17:4, 11).
3. The kingdom has been on earth since the first Pentecost following the resurrection of Christ (Col. 1:13; Rev. 1:9; Heb. 12:28).
4. The church is the kingdom the prophets saw (Dan. 2:31–44; Matt. 16:16–19).
5. Jesus will not set up an earthly kingdom (John 18:36; 17:4, 11).
6. This doctrine accuses God, Christ, the prophets, and apostles of lying (Eph. 1:3–4; 3:9–11, 21).
7. The church was in God's eternal purpose; it was not a substitute for the kingdom.
8. Neither the word *rapture* nor its teaching is found in the Bible.
9. Men have set dates for the return of Christ, but only God knows the time (Matt. 24:36).
10. If the kingdom is still future, then some folks have to be two thousand years old (Mark 9:1).
11. If the kingdom is yet future, then Jesus gave the keys to the wrong man (Matt. 16:16–19). But Jesus did give the keys to Peter and he did not die with unused keys. Peter's first gospel sermon on Pentecost made use the keys of the kingdom to which Jesus referred (Acts 2:17–47).

12. All land and seed promises have been fulfilled (Josh. 21:43; 23:14–15; Gal. 3:26–29).
13. What if the Jews reject Jesus again? Why did they reject Him the first time?
14. Jesus is now king (Acts 2:30–35; 1 Tim. 6:15). He is ruling over His kingdom!
15. People were in the kingdom in the first century (see #3 above). Premillennialists will not explain this!
16. The kingdom would be established while David "slept" (2 Sam. 7:12–13; Acts 2:29–35). David was still in the grave when the kingdom was set up. Question: If all righteous people are to be called up in the rapture before the kingdom is set up, David cannot be in the rapture.
17. The thousand years are no more literal than is the account of the beheaded ones in Revelation 20:4 being the only ones saved.
18. The beast referred to in Revelation was a king in the first century, not someone to come later (Rev. 17:9–14).

Conclusion

The Bible teaches that Jesus will return with a shout, with the voice of the archangel, and with the trump of God. The dead will rise first, the living will be changed, and all will then stand before the throne of judgment (1 Thess. 4:16–17; 1 Cor. 15:50–58; Matt. 25:31–46; John 5:28–29). To expose the rapture doctrine as false, all one must do is prove that the kingdom was established almost two thousand years ago. When that is proved, the rest of the "left behind" doctrine falls like a row of dominoes! If this doctrine sounds confusing, that is because it is. It reeks with sensationalism; it is false! No one can believe that doctrine and the Bible at the same time.

I do not know about you, but I do not want an earthly kingdom! Also, if the book of Revelation must be literally fulfilled after the rapture, then only male, virgin Jews and beheaded folks will be saved! (Rev. 14:1–5; 20:4). Yes, it is a foolish and ridiculous doctrine.

Question: Why did the Jews, according to this doctrine, reject Jesus the first time? Why did God have to "think fast" and give the church as a substitute? Why did they reject the very thing—the earthly kingdom—which they say He will set up when He returns? It makes no sense.

QUESTIONS

1. Neither the word *rapture* nor its _____ is found in the Bible.
2. The "left behind" doctrine (rapture) is commonly called "_____."
3. Simply put, this whole ridiculous scheme is designed to reach one goal: For _____ to set up an _____ _____.
4. The kingdom has been on earth since _____ (Col. 1:13; Rev. 1:9; Heb. 12:28).
5. If the _____ is still in the future, then some folks are _____ years old (Mark 9:1).
6. Jesus is now _____ (Acts 2:30–35; 1 Tim. 6:15). As king, He now _____ over a kingdom!
7. The beast was a _____ in the first _____, and not someone in the future (Rev. 17:9–14).
8. The _____ is the kingdom the prophets _____ (Dan. 2:31–44; Matt. 16:16–19).
9. If the kingdom is yet future, then Jesus gave the _____ to the wrong _____ (Matt. 16:16–19).
10. No one can believe the rapture, the "left behind" idea, and the _____ at the same time.

TRUE OR FALSE

1. ____ The doctrine of the rapture is clearly taught in the Bible.
2. ____ According to the rapture doctrine, the church was never in the mind of God.
3. ____ According to the rapture doctrine, hundred-pound hailstones will fall.
4. ____ If the rapture occurs, then only 144,000 virgin, beheaded, male Jews will be in that number.
5. ____ The Bible teaches that no one but the Father knows the time of Jesus' return.

FIVE SIMPLE QUESTIONS

1. What verse teaches that people of the first century would remain alive until the kingdom was established?
2. What verse teaches that John was in the kingdom in the first century?
3. Which verse in Matthew teaches that the church is called the kingdom?
4. What verse in Daniel teaches that the kingdom was to be established in the days of the Roman kings?
5. Which verse teaches that Paul was in the kingdom in the first century?

37

Plain Bible Talk

ABOUT RIGHTLY DIVIDING THE BIBLE

PURPOSE
To outline a general overview of the Bible.

GOAL
To be able to close our eyes and draw a straight line between Genesis and Revelation.

CHALLENGING THOUGHT
By knowing this general outline, one will "fall in love" with Bible study.

KEY WORDS
knowledge	truth	rightly dividing
study	ignorance	handling aright

CHOICES BEFORE US
One will either rightly divide the Bible or remain in spiritual ignorance.

THREE GREAT TRUTHS
The Bible was written to be understood.
The Bible can be understood.
The Bible must be understood.

SCRIPTURES TO BE READ AND STUDIED
Ephesians 3:3–4	2 Timothy 2:15; 3:16–17
Romans 10:17	Acts 20:32

PRAYER FOR TODAY
Dear God, help me to understand the Bible from Genesis to Revelation and then to teach others Thy truths.

Introduction

Second Timothy 2:15 means more than just finding all the scriptures on baptism or the Lord's supper! It also means more than just memorizing all the books of the Bible. It is time—yea, past time—that we study the Bible, and not just about the Bible. It is no surprise there is so much ignorance in the church today! The Bible, rightly divided, is a wonderful and understandable book. One cannot teach what he does not know. It is a "sure thing" that spiritual famine will come when an ignorance of the Bible prevails. We need less dependence on books by man and more on the Book of God. Many approach Bible study with little or no system whatsoever. May this study help all of us to become better acquainted with the Bible.

Forty men wrote the sixty-six books of the Bible, covering a time period of some 1,600 years of the 5,972 years since Genesis 1:1. The Bible, chronology, archaeology, and history affirm the following outline.

Rightly Dividing the Bible

1. *The Creation* (Gen. 1–5). The time covered is 1,656 years and the date is 3960–2304 BC. The theme is the creation of all things and the sin of Adam and Eve.

2. *The Flood* (Gen. 6:1–11:26). The time covered is 427 years and the date is 2304–1876 BC. The theme is the sin and fall of man, and the destruction of the earth by a world-wide flood.

3. *The Patriarchal Period* (Gen. 11:27–50:26). The time covered is 215 years and the date is 1876–1661 BC. The theme is the life of Abraham, Isaac, Jacob, and Jacob's twelve sons. (The 215 years actually end with Genesis 41:57, but the conclusion of the story of these men continues until the end of the book). Note: The book of Job should be studied here.

4. *In Egypt* (Gen. 42:1–Exod. 12:36). The time covered is 215 years and the date is 1661–1446 BC. The theme is the time spent in Egypt until their freedom to enter Canaan.

5. *In the Wilderness* (Exod. 12:37–Deut. 34:12). The time covered is 40 years and the date is 1446–1406 BC. The theme is their march toward Canaan and their entrance into that land. (Note: They could have entered the land in the second year after their departure from Egypt, but because of doubt and a distrust of God, they wandered another 38 years.)

6. *Entering Canaan* (Josh. 1–24). The time covered is seven years and the date is 1406–1399 BC. The theme is their entrance into the land and the dividing of it.

7. *The Judges* (Judg. 1:1–1 Sam. 8:22). The time covered is 350 years and the date is 1399–1050 BC. The theme is the story of the 15 judges and Israel's beginning as a nation in Canaan.

8. *The Nation United* (1 Sam. 9:1–1 Kings 11; 1 Chron. 10:1–2 Chron. 9:31). The time covered is 120 years and the date is 1050–930 BC. The theme is the history of Israel as a united nation under Saul (1050–1010 BC), David (1010–970 BC), and Solomon (970–930 BC). (Note: Psalms, Proverbs, Ecclesiastes, and Song of Solomon should be studied here.)

9. *The Nation Divided* (1 Kings 12–2 Kings 23; 2 Chron. 10–35). The 930 BC date is a fact! The time covered is 344 years and the date is 930–586 BC. (Jerusalem fell on July 18, 586 BC.) The theme is that of God's people dividing and becoming two distinct nations, Israel and Judah. Prophets were sent to both nations (2 Kings 17:13–14). Prophets to Israel: Joel, Obadiah, Jonah, Amos, Hosea, Isaiah, and Micah. Prophets to Judah: Isaiah, Micah, Nahum, Zephaniah, Jeremiah, Daniel, and Ezekiel.

10. *The Captivity* (2 Kings 24–25; 2 Chron. 36). The time covered is 70 years—actually about 67 years—and the date is 605–539 BC. The theme is Judah's captivity by Babylon. Babylon fell on October 10, 539 BC and the Jews were allowed to return to Jerusalem, their homeland.

11. *Return from Babylon* (Ezra, Nehemiah, Esther, Haggai, Zechariah, Malachi). The time covered is 107 years and the date is 538–431 BC. To organize for the departure and then the four-month journey would bring us to 538 BC. The theme is the three returns to Jerusalem: (1) to rebuild the temple, (2) to restore the law, and (3) to repair the wall. These groups were led by Zerubbabel (539 BC), Ezra (457 BC), and Nehemiah (444 BC), respectively.

12. *The Four Hundred Silent Years* (Dan. 7–12). The time covered is 431 years—actually 427 years when the four-year calendar correction is made. The date is 431 BC–AD 1. The theme is the end of the Jews' return to the birth of Christ.

13. *The Christ* (Matt. 1:18–Acts 1:11). Time covered is 33 years and the date is AD 1–33 or 4 BC–AD 29). The theme is the birth, crucifixion, burial, and resurrection of Christ.

14. *The Church* (Acts 2:1–Rev. 22:21). Time covered is 63 years and the date is AD 33–96. The theme is the establishment of the one blood-bought church and how it grew.

Note: One of the many proofs for dating is found in 1 Kings 6:1. The 480th year after Israel left Egypt is the fourth year of Solomon's reign. It is a fact that Solomon began ruling in 970. His fourth year is 966 BC. Thus, 480 plus 966 equals 1446, the time of the Exodus!

QUESTIONS

1. One will either _____ divide the Bible or remain in spiritual _____.

2. The _____ is a wonderful and _____ book if it is _____ divided.

3. We need less dependence on _____ by man and more on the Book of _____.

4. There are _____ books of the Bible and _____ different men who wrote these books.

5. The Bible was written to be _____, can be _____ and must be _____.

6. One cannot teach what he does not _____.
7. It is past time that we _____ the Bible, and not just _____ the Bible.
8. Genesis 1–5 covers _____ years.
9. Spiritual famine will surely be the result when _____ of the _____ prevails.
10. The _____, _____, _____ and _____ confirm the information in this lesson.

True or False

1. ____ The theme of Genesis 6:1–11:26 is the life of Moses.
2. ____ The Jews could have entered Canaan in the second year after their departure from Egypt.
3. ____ The fourth year of Solomon's reign was in the year 966 BC.
4. ____ The nation of Israel divided in the year AD 38.
5. ____ From Acts 2 through Revelation 22, sixty-three years passed.

Five Simple Questions

1. How many years did the Jews spend in the wilderness?
2. How many years are covered between the events of Matthew 1 and those of Acts 1?
3. How many books are in the Bible? How many writers?
4. What verse in the "Scriptures to Be Read and Studied" tells us that every scripture is inspired of God?
5. How many years was the nation of Israel united?

38

Plain Bible Talk

ABOUT EVOLUTION

PURPOSE
To expose the theory of evolution as the false teaching it is.

GOAL
To learn that the theory of evolution contradicts the foundation of the Bible.

CHALLENGING THOUGHT
What a crazy world: "Elvis is alive and God is dead!"

KEY WORDS

Bible	God	created
evolution	beginning	heavens
earth	atheist	fool

CHOICES BEFORE US
Either God made everything or dead matter evolved into man.

THREE GREAT TRUTHS
There is a God in heaven.
He made everything by the word of His mouth.
The theory of evolution is from the pits of hell!

SCRIPTURES TO BE READ AND STUDIED

Gen. 1:1–5, 6–8, 9–13	Gen. 1:14–19, 20–23
Gen. 1:24–31	Gen. 2:1–3
Psalm 14:1; 90:2	Isaiah 41:21–24
Isaiah 45:5, 12, 18	Mark 10:6
Daniel 2:28	Hebrews 3:4

PRAYER FOR TODAY
Dear God, we thank Thee for creating it all in the beginning.

Introduction

1. This study is designed to show why the common person rejects the theory of evolution. Yes, I call it a theory because the evolutionary process cannot be proved! Evolution is defined as "the hypothesis that millions of years ago, lifeless matter acted upon natural forces, and gave origin to one or more minute living organisms which have since evolved into all living and extinct plants and animals, including man." Theistic evolutionists believe that a higher power—maybe God—made it all and then let it evolve on its own. Atheistic evolution denies God—period!

2. Charles Smith, the late and former president of the *American Association for the Advancement of Atheism,* said, "In the beginning was matter, which begat the amoeba, which begat the worm, which begat the fish, which begat the amphibian, which begat the reptile, which begat the lower mammal, which begat the lemur, which begat the monkey, which begat man, who imagined God." Read Genesis 1:1 and see the simple truth of this whole matter!

3. *Evolution* is not a bad word. It means "to roll out or forth, to unfold, open out, work out, or develop gradually." Man has taken this word and distorted it, as he did the word *gay*. We need the courage and faith to believe there is a God, and also to believe God! Stand with God and you will never regret it. Evolution denies every basic truth of God!

4. Some statements from evolutionists: "Evolution is a fact. Man and ape have a common ancestor and that is a fact. Man is kin to every living thing, be it ape, flea, seaweed, or oak tree. The tape worm is a possible forty-second cousin. Even the universe evolved without God."

5. The following are two of the most powerful proofs (?) concerning the theory of evolution:

a. *Geology and paleontology, a study of the rocks and fossils.* This is really their "big gun" and yet it fizzles like a water gun! They date rocks by fossils and fossils by rocks. Makes sense, huh? A fossil is an imprint of organic matter in sediment. Yet, after examining millions of fossils, we have not a single one of an animal in the process of change! Archeologists have found humans, dogs, monkeys, cows, birds, fish, bees—you name it!—and never have they found half one and half another. The discoveries have always been fossils of fully developed animals or humans. Why? Genesis 1:1! We have found human footprints superimposed in dinosaur tracks and human and dinosaur remains side by side in the same stratum! The Cambrian Age rock is the oldest, according to evolutionists, and yet, all fossils in it are those of fully developed plants and animals! And this is their best proof? One "funny" fossil would prove their case!

b. *Anthropology, a study of man.* If evolution is true, there should be millions of skeletons of man in his intermediate stages! But again, there is not a single one! If evolution is still going on, and Darwinism says it is, why are not monkeys and apes changing into humans now? This must be the case if this ungodly theory is true! The Heidelberg man was reconstructed from one jaw bone! The Java man was reconstructed from three bones and a few teeth! The Peking man was reconstructed from one tooth! The Piltdown man was reconstructed from two bones and one tooth; the jawbone came from a ten-year-old ape! The Handy Man, so called because tools were found with his fossil remains, was reconstructed from a few bones found among tools! And this is their best proof? Truly a fool denies God and believes evolution!

Some Observations and Questions for Evolutionists

1. Explain how woman evolved.
2. How did the first baby learn to talk? Who taught it? Did death evolve?
3. If evolution developed a human baby, could it talk and survive without adult help?

4. Produce the human with a monkey face and tail, if you can. Would it be able to say half the alphabet?

5. Present concrete, tangible, and scientific proof of the origin and evolution of life.

6. Prove that evolution is taking place today.

7. Produce just one fossil of one animal in the process of changing to another.

8. If horses grew taller because they were running from tigers, why didn't the tigers become faster by chasing the horses.

9. What was the pre-bee? Was it a regular bee or something else?

10. How did man survive if his respiratory system did not develop until late in the evolutionary process, millions of years after man started evolving? How did he breathe?

11. What kind of explosion would it take to produce a watch, car, or house?

12. Why can't man create life? Why will he never create life?

13. If the days of Genesis 1 were actually long epochs of time, then so are days 8, 10, and 15. Then just how old was Adam when he died at the age of 930? (Gen. 5:5).

14. If someone believes evolution is true, is he not saying that Jesus was the son of a monkey?

15. Does a half ape and half man have a half soul? Where did he get this half soul?

16. Produce proof that the earth is millions of years old, not 5,973 years old, as the Bible says.

17. Plants evolved on the third day, and a day was thousands of years long, according to evolutionists. How did they survive to the sixth day when insects evolved? Partially developed insects cannot pollinate plants.

18. A cow can mate with a buffalo and produce a cattalo and a donkey with a zebra and produce a zeonkey because those animal are of the same kind, respectively. But if a fish were to mate with a bird, what should we call the offspring?

19. Why isn't non-living matter in warm seas continually evolving into living matter?

20. If every book on evolution were lost or destroyed, name one important scientific fact that would be lost. A cat will never give birth to a duck. God said so! (Gen. 1:11–12, 24).

QUESTIONS

1. Either _____ made everything or dead matter evolved into _____.

2. Truly, the theory of _____ is from the _____ of hell!

3. Evolution denies every basic _____ of God.

4. A _____ is an imprint in sediment or _____ matter.

5. The _____ man was constructed from three bones and a few teeth.

6. If every single book on evolution was lost or destroyed, name ____ important fact that would be _____.

7. Can a watch, _____ or _____ just happen by an explosion?

8. Truly, a _____ denies God and believes in _____!

9. We need the _____ and _____ to believe there is a God and also, to _____ God!

10. A _____ will never give birth to a duck.

TRUE OR FALSE

1. ____ The theory of evolution is taught throughout the Bible.

2. ____ Fossils have been found showing a monkey changing into a man.

3. ____ Evolution teaches the days in Genesis 1 were long periods of time.

4. ____ The bee has always been a bee.

5. ____ Evolution teaches that man is a cousin to the tape worm.

FIVE SIMPLE QUESTIONS

1. Can a watch, car, or house result from an explosion? Why?

2. What does God call the person who denies Him?

3. According to the Bible, how old is the earth as of 2013?

4. If evolution is true, then Jesus is a son of what animal?

5. Can the theory of the evolutionary be proved? Why?

39

Plain Bible Talk

ABOUT THE
BAPTIST CHURCH

PURPOSE
To show the differences between the church of Christ and the Baptist church.

GOAL
To learn these major differences and then teach others.

CHALLENGING THOUGHT
Contrary to popular belief, John the Baptist was not a Baptist preacher.

KEY WORDS

one	Bible	Roger Williams
manuals	Christ	John Smyth
baptism	truth	

CHOICES BEFORE US
Either the Bible is right when it states there is but one church or it is wrong and the ways of men are right.

THREE GREAT TRUTHS
There is only one blood-bought church.
That church began on the Pentecost of Acts 2.
No man-made church has the scriptural right to
    exist.

SCRIPTURES TO BE READ AND STUDIED
Matthew 16:18   Acts 20:28; 2:38–47
Romans 16:16   Ephesians 4:4–6

PRAYER FOR TODAY
Dear God, we thank Thee for the one blood-bought church.

Introduction

This lesson is designed to inform members of the church of Christ about the beliefs of friends, relatives, and neighbors in the Baptist church. There are various divisions of the Baptist church: Freewill, Landmark, Seventh Day, Missionary, Primitive, General, and Southern to name a few. For the most part, they are in fellowship with one another. This lesson is not intended to be vindictive or spiteful toward anyone associated with the Baptist church but simply to present some of the major beliefs of that denomination. This material is confirmed by their own preachers, authors, and historians.

Is the Baptist Church the Church Jesus Built?

To be quite frank, no! Here are some facts about the church Jesus built:

- It was purposed before the foundation of the world (Eph. 1:3–4; 3:9–11).
- It was prophesied by inspired prophets (Dan. 2:44; Isa. 2:1–4).
- It was promised by the Lord Himself (Matt. 16:18).
- It was prepared for by servants of God, including John the Baptist (Matt. 3:1–3).
- It was perfected—became a reality—in the city of Jerusalem in AD 33 (Acts 2:1–47).
- It belongs to Christ and could not have been named after a single act of obedience (Rom. 16:16).
- It is the only church Jesus purchased with His blood (Acts 20:28; Eph. 1:22–23; 4:4).
- It has Jesus as its only head (Col. 1:18).

Question: If saved people were added to Christ's church in the first century, then why did man think we needed other churches? (Acts 2:38–47). Please answer.

The Baptist Church

The Baptist church movement began in London in 1607. It was organized in Holland in 1609. John Smyth, along with others—among them Thomas Helwys—founded the Baptist church. That denomination grew out of Mennonite and Separatists movements, those who wanted a complete break with the Church of England. The first Baptist church in the United States was founded in 1639 in Providence, Rhode Island, by Roger Williams.

Some Differences Between Bible Doctrine and Baptist Doctrine
1. The name, church of Christ (Matt. 16:18; Rom. 16:16).
   The name, Baptist Church (Scripture: _____).
2. The founder is Christ (Matt. 16:18; Acts 20:28).
   The founder is John Smyth (Scripture: _____).
3. The place of origin is Jerusalem (Isa. 2:1–4; Acts 2:1–5).
   The place of origin is Holland (Scripture: _____).
4. The date of origin is AD 33 (Dan. 2:44; Acts 2:1–5).
   The date of origin is AD 1609 (Scripture: _____).
5. The standard of authority is the Bible (2 Tim. 3:16–17; John 12:48; Gal. 4:30).
   The standard of authority is Hiscox's and Pendleton's manual (Scripture: _____).
6. The Lord's supper is observed every Sunday (Acts 20:7).
   The Lord's supper is observed monthly, quarterly, or annually (Scripture: _____).
7. The singing in worship is without the mechanical instrument (Eph. 5:19; Col. 3:16).
   The singing in worship is with the mechanical instrument (Scripture: _____).
8. Baptism is essential for salvation (Acts 2:38, 47; 22:16; Gal. 3:27; 1 Pet. 3:21).

Baptism is not essential for salvation (Scripture:_____).

9. "Faith only" can justify no one (James 2:17, 19–20, 24).
   "Faith only" justifies the sinner (Scripture: _____).
10. Saved people can fall from grace (1 Cor. 10:8, 12; Gal. 5:4).
    Saved people cannot fall from grace (Scripture: _____).
11. The new birth includes water (John 3:3–5).
    The new birth does not include water (Scripture: _____).
12. Obedience to Jesus' commands is necessary for salvation (John 14:15; Heb. 5:8–9).
    Obedience to Jesus' commands is not necessary. Just accept Jesus as your personal Savior (Scripture: _____).
13. The Lord adds the saved to the church (Acts 2:38, 41, 47).
    People join the church, if they can be voted in (Scripture: _____).
14. There is only one name by which there is salvation, and that is Christ's name (Acts 4:9–12).
    There is nothing in a name, so one name is as good as another (Scripture: _____).
15. Christ is the savior of the church (Eph. 5:23; Eph. 4:4).
    Christ will save those outside that one church (Scripture: _____).

Note the absence of Bible authority for these Baptist doctrines!

QUESTIONS

1. Contrary to popular belief, _____ the _____ was not a _____ preacher.
2. The church that Jesus built was _____ before the _____ of the world.
3. The first Baptist Church in the United States was founded by _____ _____ in _____ _____, in the year _____.
4. In what year was the Baptist Church organized? _____
   Where? _____
5. Christ is the _____ of the church (Eph. 5:23).
6. According to Baptist doctrine, baptism is _____ essential to _____.

7. There is only _____ name by which there is salvation, and that name is _____ name.
8. Obedience to Jesus' _____ is necessary for salvation.
9. No man-made _____ has the scriptural right to _____.
10. If saved people were _____ to this church—the one purchased in the first century with Christ's blood (Acts 2:38–47)—then why did man think we needed other _____?

TRUE OR FALSE

1. ____ Roger Williams is the founder of the Baptist church in the United States.
2. ____ James 2:24 states that one can be saved by faith only.
3. ____ The one true New Testament church had its beginning in Jerusalem in the year A.D. 33.
4. ____ According to 1 Corinthians 10:8–12 and Galatians 5:4, one cannot fall from grace.
5. ____ The church that Jesus built was purchased with the blood of Roger Williams.

FIVE SIMPLE QUESTIONS

1. In what year did the Baptist church "movement" have its beginning?
2. In what year was the Baptist church organized?
3. What verse in the New Testament states Jesus' promise to build His church?
4. What verse in the New Testament states that baptism saves us?
5. Which Bible verse states that a person living in the Christians Age can be saved outside the one blood-bought church?

40

Plain Bible Talk

ABOUT PSALM 119

PURPOSE
To learn more about the "heart of the Bible" chapter.

GOAL
To learn that the Bible will supply all our spiritual needs.

CHALLENGING THOUGHT
All but two of the 176 verses have a specific reference to the Bible.

KEY WORDS

scriptures	precepts	testimonies
statutes	ordinances	commandments
law	word	

CHOICES BEFORE US
One will either apply the truths of Psalm 119 or fail in life.

THREE GREAT TRUTHS
One should stand in awe of the Bible.
The Bible is the sum of God's truths.
One must apply God's Word with the whole heart.

SCRIPTURES TO BE READ AND STUDIED
Psalm 119:2, 38, 46   Psalm 119:86, 89, 104, 120
Psalm 119:128, 136   Psalm 119:160, 161, 172

PRAYER FOR TODAY
Dear God, we thank Thee for Thy holy, divine, and precious words.

There are 176 verses in Psalm 119, and every one of them except two has a direct reference to the Scriptures. This psalm has rightly been called the heart of the Bible. There are 22 letters in the Hebrew alphabet and each letter heads a block of eight verses that teach a specific lesson concerning the scriptures. A knowledge of Psalm 119 will greatly increase the basic faith of a Christian. Note the key word that describes each lesson.

1. Verses 1–8: "Seek God with all your heart." Key word: *seek* (v. 2). Seeking involves attendance, giving, singing, praying, studying, the Lord's supper, and living for Him each day. Seeking God with the whole heart is the only way to please Him. Seeking requires intense effort.

2. Verses 9–16: "Allow the word to dwell in your heart." Key word: *heart* (v. 11). Having the word in our hearts is the only way we can experience real joy and happiness. His word must control our hearts (thinking).

3. Verses 17–24: "The scriptures will open your eyes." Key word: *behold* (v. 18). By beholding the scriptures, our eyes are opened to what God wants. Thus, we become better husbands, fathers, wives, mothers, children, preachers, elders, and deacons.

4. Verses 25–32: "Choose the ways of God and cleave to them." Key word: *cleave* (v. 31 ASV). We must choose the ways of God, hold on to them, and make our stand for truth.

5. Verses 33–40: "Hunger for God's word." Key word: *longed* (v. 40). Spiritual hunger will prevent us from "re-thinking" the one church, baptism, and salvation. We will become grounded in truth!

6. Verses 41–48: " Love every word of God." Key word: *love* (v. 48). Demand more than "locker room pep talks" from the pulpit. Demand book, chapter, and verse! Love the scriptures.

7. Verses 49–56: "Real comfort comes from the scriptures." Key word: *comfort* (v. 50). The scriptures give us hope and comfort. Why? They are God's breathed words! Read verse 49.

8. Verses 57–64: "The Bible will sustain us when all else fails." Key word: *righteous* (v. 62). The ways of God are always right and they will always sustain and keep us. They will not fail us!

9. Verses 65–72: "The scriptures will help us in good times and bad." Key word: *better* (v. 72). Whether good or terrible days, the Bible is better than gold, silver, things, and glory!

10. Verses 73–80: "The Bible provides wisdom." Key word: *understanding* (v. 73). As we study and gain knowledge, we must pray for wisdom to rightly divide and understand the Bible.

11. Verses 81–88: "The Bible is faithful." Key word: *faithful* (v. 86). The Bible does not contain errors, mistakes, or contradictions! You can count on the Scriptures to be what it claims.

12. Verses 89–96: "The Bible cannot be changed." Key word: *settled* (v. 89). Read Proverbs 30:6 and Revelation 22:18–19. We must change people and not the Bible.

13. Verses 97–104: "The scriptures are sweet." Key word: *taste* (v. 103). There is nothing sweeter on our tongues than God's infallible Word! The world must hear scriptures from us.

14. Verses 105–112: "The scriptures light our paths." Key word: *light* (v. 105). The Bible will keep us in the paths of right so we will know every false way (v. 110).

15. Verses 113–120: "We must fear God and His Word." Key word: *fear* (v. 120). Many no longer fear God (Job 23:15–16). As Job, we must tremble before Him. He means what He says!

16. Verses 121–128: "The Bible is always right." Key word: *right* (v. 128). The Bible is right on every subject it addresses. Name a subject and the Bible will provide truth on that subject (Gal. 4:30).

17. Verses 129–136: "Be sad over those who reject the Bible." Key word: *sadness* (v. 136). Humanism, liberalism, immorality, and denominationalism have rejected God's Word. It is sad!

18. Verses 137–144: "The Bible is the only source of truth." Key word: *truth* (v. 142). Nothing but the Bible is truth (John 8:32, 17:17). We must study the Bible, not about the Bible!

19. Verses 145–152: "Refusing the Bible means one is far from God." Key word: *far* (v. 150). When in trouble, read the Bible (v. 148). The Bible draws us near to God (147).

20. Verses 153–160: "The Bible is the sum of God's divine truth." Key word: *sum* (v. 160 ASV).Not only can we count on the Bible, but it also will be the standard of judgment (John 12:48).

21. Verses 161–168: "The Bible will give us peace of mind." Key word: *peace* (v. 165). God is good, great, and holy. We can have absolute peace when we love and obey His Word!

22. Verses 169–176 "Salvation is found in the scriptures." Key word: *salvation* (v. 174). When our days on earth come to an end, the only thing that really matters is to die in the Lord! God is our one and only hope. There is an eternity and I want to be with God!

QUESTIONS

1. The Bible is the _____ of God's truths.
2. Seeking God with the _____ heart is the only way to please Him.
3. The scriptures give us _____ and comfort.
4. The Bible does not contain errors, _____ or _____!
5. We must change _____ and not the Bible.
6. The Bible will keep us in the paths of _____ and thus, we will know every _____ way.
7. The _____ is right on every subject.
8. We must study the _____, not about the Bible.
9. We can have absolute _____ when we love and _____ His word!
10. God is our one and only _____.

TRUE OR FALSE

1. ____ Psalm 119 is unique in that it never refers to the Scriptures, commandments, and such like.
2. ____ The Bible contains many errors and contradictions.
3. ____ One must allow the Bible to control one's heart (thinking).
4. ____ The Bible is right on every subject it addresses.
5. ____ According to Psalms 119:89, the Bible can be changed, revised and altered.

FIVE SIMPLE QUESTIONS

1. When our days on earth come to an end, what is the only thing that will really matter?
2. What set of eight verses in our lesson teaches us to hunger for the Bible?
3. As we study the Bible, for what must we pray in addition to knowledge?
4. According to Job 23:15–16, was Job afraid of God? Why?
5. How many verses are in Psalm 119?

41

Plain Bible Talk

ABOUT INDIVIDUAL RESPONSIBILITY

PURPOSE
To learn about my responsibility as a child of God.

GOAL
To maintain and practice this responsibility.

CHALLENGING THOUGHT
One-half of new converts fall away and never return.

KEY WORDS

Christian	attitude	responsibility
love	dedication	commitment
faithful		

CHOICES BEFORE US
Either a person will grow in Christ, remain faithful, and go to heaven, or he will be lost in hell because he allows Satan to have his way.

THREE GREAT TRUTHS
One will never regret becoming a Christian.
The Christian life is the best life of all.
A Christian has help from God, Christ, and faithful brethren.

SCRIPTURES TO BE READ AND STUDIED

2 Peter 3:18   Revelation 2:10
2 Corinthians 5:17   Philippians 4:13
Matthew 22:36–37

PRAYER FOR TODAY
Dear God, I thank Thee beyond measure for allowing me to be Thy child.

Introduction

Each Christian has the responsibility to exert the proper influence by his life, words, deeds, and dress. The world is watching and we must accept the challenge (1 Cor. 4:9). Please read Zechariah 8:23. The world is begging for Christian examples.

With much joy and great love we welcome new Christians into the one true New Testament church, the church of Christ (Rom. 16:16), the one for which our Lord died. When a person obeys the gospel, Christ becomes the Lord, Master, and ruler of his life. What a privilege to be a part of God's family, the church (1 Tim. 3:15), with brothers and sisters who share a unique bond of love. Knowing that our souls will live forever, we encourage and help one another to go to heaven. Just one glimpse of Jesus coming in glory will make all the trials and heartaches of this life worthwhile.

A person can choose from hundreds of man-made churches, but the Bible tells of only one blood-bought church. By the grace, mercy, and love of God we were baptized for the remission of sins and added to that one church (Acts 2:38; 2:47).

Making a better world and allowing the church to be what God wants starts with each individual Christian. Note the following ten truths which will help us fulfill our responsibilities as Christians. We will never have to apologize for being a Christian! We will please the Master if we develop and maintain these simple and sacred truths.

1. *I will develop and maintain the Christian attitude* (Matt. 5:1–12). That assumes total commitment to Christ (Matt. 6:33), allowing the Bible to control my thinking. I will never have to brag about my righteousness because my life will be proof of such (2 Tim. 2:19).

2. *I have God in my daily walk and Jesus will be my ever-constant friend* (Heb. 13:5–6). I can now call God my Father. I also have many brothers and sisters who will help carry my burdens and heartaches. Christians should be my best friends!

3. *I am a new creature, a changed person, and a servant of God* (2 Cor. 5:17). I now have new desires, aspirations, way of dress, views, talk, and habits. Jesus is my everything.

4. *I now know that I can make it to heaven, and if I fail to do so, I have no one to blame but myself* (Phil. 4:13). Nothing can keep me from my desired goal (Rom. 8:28–39). Heaven is worth it all. This earthly life offers a short time of preparation for that eternal abode.

5. *I will still have problems and disappointments because God never promised immunity from such.* The peace that stems from my faith in God and His Word will carry me through (Phil. 4:7). God promises to see me through anything the world throws at me.

6. *I have made my stand with God and determined to be faithful in attendance to all services.* I will pray and study the Bible daily. I want Jesus to be formed in me (Gal. 4:19). I will defeat Satan in my Christian life by being happy, standing for truth, and winning souls!

7. *I vow to use all my talents to God's glory and honor* (Tit. 3:1). I will take pride in God's local congregation, pray for it, support it, and defend it. I will do all I can—and then some! I want my neighbors to see Jesus in me.

8. *I will make my stand for the right and against the wrong* (Eph. 6:13). I will do nothing if there is not book, chapter, and verse authority for that act. I will keep myself pure and never purposely hurt or harm my family or the church.

9. *I know there will be times when my family, friends, and foes will speak evil of me and the church.* With love, boldness, kindness, and truth I will maintain my Christian identity and tell them what the Bible says concerning their questions or accusations (Luke 6:26). I will determine to be God's mirror and His spokesman.

10. *I will love God with all my heart, soul, and mind* (Matt. 22:36–37). God will not accept anything less! I will keep my focus on the blood-

stained cross and daily thank my heavenly Father for His unspeakable gift (2 Cor. 9:15).

QUESTIONS

1. A _____ has help from God, Christ, and _____ brethren.
2. Each Christian has the responsibility to exert the proper _____ by his _____, _____, _____ and dress.
3. What a privilege to be a part of God's _____, the _____.
4. We are _____ and _____, and share a unique _____ of _____.
5. By the _____, mercy and love of _____, we were _____ for the remission of _____ (Acts 2:38) and added to that _____ church (Acts 2:47).
6. I will never have to "_____" about my _____ because my life will be _____ of such.
7. Christians should be my best _____!
8. I now have new _____, _____, _____ of dress, views, _____ and _____.
9. I will still have problems and _____ because God has never promised _____ from such.
10. I want Jesus to be _____ in me (Gal. 4:19).

TRUE OR FALSE

1. ____ According to Luke 6:26, everybody will speak well of a Christian.
2. ____ According to Matthew 22:36–37, one must love himself above others and God.
3. ____ According to 1 Timothy 3:15, the church is the house of God.
4. ____ According to 1 Corinthians 4:9, others are watching and observing the Christian.
5. ____ According to 2 Timothy 2:19, the Christian must always tell others of his righteousness.

FIVE SIMPLE QUESTIONS

1. Seeing what event will make all the trials and heartaches of this life worthwhile?
2. For what is the world begging?
3. Who is God's unspeakable gift?
4. What verse in 2 Corinthians says the Christian is a new creature?
5. Give scriptural proof that nothing can separate us from the love of God.

42

Plain Bible Talk

ABOUT THE PERFECT PLAN OF REDEMPTION

PURPOSE
To learn why God's plan to save man is perfect.

GOAL
To study fifteen reasons this plan is perfect.

CHALLENGING THOUGHT
Everything God does is perfect.

KEY WORDS
purposed   prophesied   promised
prepared   perfected

CHOICES BEFORE US
Either God's plan of redemption is accepted for what it claims to be or the Bible is a fake.

THREE GREAT TRUTHS
God is perfect.
His plan to save man is perfect.
Jesus is perfect.

SCRIPTURES TO BE READ AND STUDIED
Matthew 5:48   1 Peter 2:21–22
James 1:25   Deuteronomy 32:4
Job 37:16

PRAYER FOR TODAY
Dear God, we recognize Thee and all Thy ways as being perfect, and we thank Thee for it.

Introduction

God devised a perfect plan to save man. He chose the right time for Christ to come into the world and to die on the cross (Gal. 4:4). Jesus' sacrifice did not happen by chance! God had so planned it before the foundation of the world (Eph. 1:3–4; 3:9–12). How did all this come to work together? Answer: Because of the perfect God! The blood-bought church is the end result of God's masterful scheme of redemption (Acts 2:38–47; 20:28; Rom. 16:16). Every person, place, and thing found in the Bible was a part of this plan coming to pass. Every prophesy of Christ in the Old Testament—over 300 of them—came to pass (Acts 13:29). God is the one and only great God (Isa. 45:5, 12, 18; Dan. 2:28; 3:17; 4:25).

God Is Great and Perfect

1. God is perfect (Job 37:16; Matt. 5:48).
2. God's ways are perfect (2 Sam. 22:31).
3. God's law is perfect (Ps. 19:7; James 1:25).
4. God's knowledge is perfect (Job 37:16).
5. God's works are perfect (Deut. 32:4).

The Perfect Plan Came Together Because

1. There was a perfect planner (Matt. 5:48; Eph. 3:9–12).
2. There was a perfect builder (Matt. 16:18; 1 Pet. 2:21–22).
3. There was a perfect sacrifice (1 Pet. 1:18–19).
4. There is a perfect head (Col. 1:18).
5. There is a perfect foundation (1 Cor. 3:11).
6. There is a perfect name (Acts 4:12; Rom. 16:16; Phil. 2:10–11).
7. There is a perfect law (James 1:25).
8. There is a perfect plan of salvation (Mark 16:16; Acts 2:38–47).
9. There is a perfect worship (John 4:23–24).
10. There is a perfect organization (Phil. 1:1).

11. There is a perfect plan of finance (1 Cor. 16:1–2).
12. There is a perfect example for us to follow (1 Pet. 2:21–22).
13. There are perfect blessings found in the perfect Savior (Eph. 1:3).
14. There is a perfect home awaiting the redeemed (John 14:1–3).
15. There will be a perfect judgment (John 12:48; Matt. 25:31–46).

Conclusion

1. *Why am I a member of the church of Christ?*
   I read about it in the Bible (Rom. 16:16).
2. *What drew me to the church of Christ?*
   The fifteen reasons stated above!
3. *Why do I defend the church of Christ?*
   Because it was bought with the blood of Christ!
4. *Why do I preach there is but one blood-bought church?*
   Because the Bible tells me so!
5. *Why do I proclaim that the church of Christ is worth fighting for and that it is the culmination of God's masterful plan of redemption?*

   Because as a Christian, God expects me to do so, and He will accept no less!

QUESTIONS

1. Either God's plan of _____ is accepted for what it claims to be or the _____ is a fake.
2. Every _____, _____ and thing found in the Bible was a part of this _____ coming to pass.
3. God is the _____, great and only _____.
4. God is _____. His plan to save _____ is perfect. Jesus is _____.
5. He (God) chose the "right" time for _____ to come into the world and to _____ on the _____.
6. The blood-bought _____ is the end result of God's _____ scheme of _____.
7. Everything God does is _____.
8. Every _____ of Christ in the _____ _____ (over 300) came to pass.
9. God had this plan in His _____ before the _____ of the world.
10. God laid a _____ plan to save man.

TRUE OR FALSE

1. ____ One can read about the church of Christ in the Bible.
2. ____ Heaven is the perfect home for all the redeemed.
3. ____ According to Philippians 1:1, popes, high priests, and doctors are a part of the church's organization.
4. ____ According to Matthew 25:31–46 there will be a judgment for some, but not for everyone.
5. ____ God gave us an imperfect law.

FIVE SIMPLE QUESTIONS

1. Was Jesus the perfect sacrifice? Support your answer.
2. What scripture says all spiritual blessings are found in Christ?
3. How many names did God give by which we are saved? Give scripture.
4. Who is the perfect builder of the church? Give scripture.
5. What verse states that Jesus is the head of the church?

43

Plain Bible Talk

ABOUT THE
BOOK OF REVELATION

PURPOSE
To present a general overview of the book of Revelation.

GOAL
To allow John to explain the book of Revelation to us.

CHALLENGING THOUGHT
The book can be understood if we view it through first-century eyes.

KEY WORDS

God	Satan	Christ
beast	Domitian	churches
victory	death	persecution

CHOICES BEFORE US
Either the book of Revelation can be understood or God lied (Rev. 1:3).

THREE GREAT TRUTHS
John wrote the book between AD 69–79 during the reign of Emperor Vespasian.

The book is addressed to the seven churches of Asia Minor.

He told them that relief from their persecution was coming soon.

SCRIPTURES TO BE READ AND STUDIED

Rev. 1:1–4, 11   Rev. 2:10; 6:9–11
Rev. 17:9–12   Rev. 20:11–15
Rev. 22:6–7, 10, 12, 20

PRAYER FOR TODAY
*Dear God, please use me to keep pure the one church
for which my Lord died.*

Introduction

The book of Revelation—not Revelations!—is probably the most abused and misused book in the Bible. Its 22 chapters and 404 verses can easily be understood. Give John time to explain his visions; listen to him and not to some educated, uninspired man. Dismiss the ideas of your favorite preacher or commentary. Never apply the truths of Revelation to another people, time, or purpose except that which the context demands. John is writing to the persecuted Christians of the first century, telling them that God is aware of their troubles and will soon take care of them. Always accept the truth behind the visions. Ask as you read each vision: What is the lesson taught here? God, as it were, pulls the curtain back and marches visions across the stage for John to see, write down, and send to the seven churches in Asia Minor (1:4, 11), all of which were churches of Christ (Matt. 16:18; Eph. 1:22–23; 4:4; Rom. 16:16). The book is progressive. Each chapter naturally and chronologically follows the preceding one.

A simple outline of the book:

Chapters 1–3: Introduction
Chapters 4–11: The message of the seven seals.
Chapters 12–20: The spiritual battle of the book
Chapters 21–22: Victory for the church

Understanding Revelation and Its Lessons

1. John writes to the seven churches (1:1–4, 11). Lesson: As John waited for God's message, so must we (Isa. 40:30–31; Gal. 4:30; Ps. 119:128). If not, we cause trouble in the church.

2. The seven churches are named and their spiritual conditions are discussed (chs. 2–3). Five were unfaithful and two were faithful.
Lesson: Keep the church pure (Rev. 2:10; Mark 4:19; 2 Tim. 2:2).

3. God made all things (4:1–8) and He controls His creation (4:9–11). The churches needed this reminder!
Lesson: There is only one God (Isa. 45:5) and He rules (Dan. 4:25).

4. God holds a book in His hand which contains the message to the churches (5:1–8). Jesus is worthy by His shed blood to reveal the contents (9–14).
Lesson: There is only one blood-bought church (Acts 20:28, Rom. 16:16; Eph. 1:22–23; 4:4).

5. The church is being persecuted but God promises relief (6:9–11, 17).
Lesson: Brethren, make a stand for the right and against the wrong (Eph. 6:13–18). Trust God even in times of the greatest temptation!

6. The devil used his full package of tricks and failed. The faithful will stand victorious with the Master (7:9–17).
Lesson: Faithful Christians will be able to stand (Mark 16:16).

7. God calls for the enemy to stop the persecuting (chs. 8–9) but Rome refuses (9:21).
Lesson: We must put repentance back into our preaching (Acts 2:38; 8:22).

8. God said Rome had sinned away the opportunity to repent (10:4, 6). She will see God's wrath!
Lesson: Do not sin away the day of grace (2 Cor. 5:10). There are no changes after death!

9. God promises to protect the church during His dealings with Rome (11:1, 15).
Lesson: God is concerned about His church and will protect it. Do not tamper with God's authority (Hos. 5:10).

10. Satan failed at the birth and the crucifixion of Christ, but he continues to try to destroy the church (12:17).
Lesson: We can defeat Satan by using God's Word (Matt. 4:10).

11. John says the church's enemy is a beast. (13:1–2, 4, 7).

Lesson: We must also identify the enemies of the cross (Phil. 3:18). Peace, unity, and fellowship must be based on truth!

12. By faithfully and obediently following Jesus, they defeated the beast and received the crown (14:1–5, 13).
Lesson: Dying in the Lord is the only thing that really matters (Rev. 14:13).

13. Judgment day came for Rome (chs. 15–16).
Lesson: The wrath of God must be preached from our pulpits. If hell were preached in today's cathedrals, the walls would crack! (Matt. 25:31–46).

14. God plainly reveals the identity of the persecuting beast, Emperor Domitian (17:9–12).
Lesson: The Bible can and must be understood (Ps. 119:89, 128, 160–161).

15. God warns His people not to fellowship Rome or partake of her sins (18:4).
Lesson: Christians are to avoid some people, places, and things (Eph. 5:11).

16. God kept His promise to judge Rome and make the church victorious (19:2, 7–17).
Lesson: God can still be trusted to keep His promises (Tit. 1:2).

17. God shows John a vision in which the martyred saints are rewarded (20:4–6).
Lesson: We will also be found in the Book of Life if we are faithful till death (2:10; 20:11–15).

18. God pictures the church in a new setting and away from Rome's persecution (21:2, 9, 10; 22:17–19).
Lesson: If we are striving to receive the crown, we must not tamper with the Bible (22:18–19).

QUESTIONS

1. The book can be understood if we view it through "_____ _____" eyes.
2. One must give _____ time to explain the _____ given to him.
3. God made all _____ and He is in _____ of them.
4. The church is being _____, but God promises _____.
5. God calls for the enemy (_____) to stop the persecuting, but they _____.
6. Satan failed at the _____ and _____ of Christ and now tries to destroy the_____.
7. _____, _____ and fellowship must be based on _____!
8. Dying in the _____ is the only thing that really _____.
9. There are some _____, _____ and things that Christians are to _____.
10. God will keep His _____ and He can be _____.

TRUE OR FALSE

1. ____ Seven congregations are mentioned in chapters 2 and 3.
2. ____ We can defeat Satan by using God's Word.
3. ____ Rome is the enemy that is persecuting the church in the book of Revelation.
4. ____ We do not know who wrote the book of Revelation.
5. ____ According to Revelation 1:3, the book cannot be understood.

FIVE SIMPLE QUESTIONS

1. To whom did John write the book of Revelation?
2. According to 17:9–11, when did John write this book?
3. Did John tell them that relief from persecution was soon coming? Prove your answer.
4. What verse in chapter 13 says the beast (Domitian) would persecute the saints?
5. Who was worthy to take the book from God's hand?

44

Plain Bible Talk

ABOUT THE WORD *IF*

PURPOSE
To reveal the weakness of the word *if*.

GOAL
To study how eternally dangerous it is to rely on the little word *if*.

CHALLENGING THOUGHT
If is one of the weakest words in our vocabulary.

KEY WORDS

weak	dangerous	weasel
habit	useless	hard
difficult		

CHOICES BEFORE US
One will either accept the Bible or use the word *if* and deny it.

THREE GREAT TRUTHS
If never preached a sermon.
If never saved a soul.
If never brought back a day.

SCRIPTURES TO BE READ AND STUDIED

John 11:21	Numbers 22:18, 34
2 Samuel 19:6	

Prayer for Today
Dear God, help me to avoid using if *as a reason to disobey Thee.*

Introduction

The word *if* is not always used in a negative manner. However, the study today will show that the word is often used as an excuse for not obeying the Bible. *If* is often used as a weasel word—no backbone, no courage, and no respect to do or say it like it is. Some of the hardest and most difficult words to preach are small three-letter words such as *sin, but, the, one,* and *for.* The religious world is divided over these simple three-letter words. An old saying goes like this:

If *ifs, ands,* and *buts* were candy and nuts,
What a wonderful world this would be.

How true that is!

The Word If

1. *If* is one of the weakest and most dangerous words that comes across our tongues.
2. *If* starts one out on the wrong course and is the epitaph of millions.
3. *If* is a marking over the portals of the city of the lost! *If* never changed a death!
4. *If*, attached to one of God's commands, makes God's will futile and useless.
5. *If* discounts and discredits the wonderful providence of God.
6. *If* never broke a habit, saved a soul, planted a garden, or brought back a second of time.

Examples of the Wrong Way to Use If

If my aunt Jane had a mustache, she would be my uncle George! If a frog had wings, he would not be bumping his belly on the ground all the time! In John 11:21, Martha said that if Jesus had been there, Lazarus would not have died. But Jesus was not there! So *if* did not change what had happened! How many times have we heard, "If I had gone a different route" or "If only I had left two minutes earlier" or "If I had used a different doctor" or "If only I had invested in that stock"? "If Absalom had lived" (2 Sam. 19:6), but he was dead. Many are like Balaam. They have an *if* attached to their religion. (God had already warned Balaam: Numbers 22:18, 34). Many in man-made churches say, "If the church of Christ did not have Acts 20:7, they could not prove that the Lord's supper is to be observed every week." Talk about using that dangerous and weak word *if*! The fact is, it is in the Bible and there is no *if* about it, and they must deal with God concerning this matter! There must be no *if*s attached to our obedience and service to God!

If That Verse Was Not in the Bible

1. Genesis 1:1. It is in the Bible and it forever destroys the very foundation of atheism.
2. Isaiah 7:14. It is in the Bible and it destroys modernism and agnosticism.
3. Daniel 2:44. It is in the Bible and it destroys denominationalism.
4. Revelation 22:18–19. It is in the Bible and it destroys liberalism.
5. Colossians 3:17. It is in the Bible and it destroys creeds, disciplines, and manuals of men.
6. Romans 1:26–32. It is in the Bible and it destroys the acceptance of homosexuality.
7. 1 Timothy 3:1–7; Titus 1: 5–11. It is in the Bible and it destroys the teaching that a man does not have to meet every qualification to be God's elder.
8. Acts 2:38. It is in the Bible and it destroys the sectarian preacher's objection to baptism.
9. Romans 16:16. It is in the Bible and it destroys every man-made name for every man-made church.
10. Matt. 19:1–9. It is in the Bible and it destroys the teaching that there are many reasons for divorce and remarriage.
11. 2 Timothy 4:2. It is in the Bible and it destroys the notion that preachers can use locker room pep talks, book reviews, jokes, or entertainment as sermons!
12. 1 Timothy 2:8–12. It is in the Bible and it destroys the idea that a person can dress immodestly, whether in or out of worship services.

Questions

1. The word *if* is one of the _____ words in our vocabulary.
2. *If* never _____ a sermon, _____ a soul or brought back a _____.
3. *If* starts one on the _____ course and is the _____ of millions.
4. To attach an _____ to any of God's commands makes them _____ and useless.
5. There must be no "if" attached to our _____ and _____ to God!
6. _____ said that if Jesus had been there, _____ would not have died.
7. Many in man-made churches say, "If the _____ ___ _____ did not have Acts 20:7 in the Bible, they could not prove that the _____ _____ is to be observed every week."
8. *If* discounts and discredits the _____ of God.
9. *If* is a marking over the _____ of the city of _____!
10. *If* never broke a _____, saved a _____, planted a _____ nor brought back one _____.

True or False

1. ____ Genesis 1:1 destroys the foundation of atheism.
2. ____ Romans 1:26–32 sanctions and condones homosexuality.
3. ____ Matthew 19:1–9 teaches there are many reasons for divorce and remarriage.
4. ____ Revelation 22:18–19 supports liberalism.
5. ____ Acts 2:38 destroys the sectarian preacher's objection to baptism.

Five Simple Questions

1. What verse commands the preacher to preach the word?
2. What verse destroys every man-made name for every man-made church?
3. What verse destroys liberalism?
4. What verse destroys creeds, disciplines, and manuals of men?
5. What verse destroys the acceptance of immodest dress?

45

Plain Bible Talk

ABOUT TEACHING
THE NEXT GENERATION

PURPOSE
To know, accept, and fulfill our responsibility in teaching the next generation.

GOAL
To study specific things that must be passed on to the next generation.

CHALLENGING THOUGHT
We have only eighteen short years at most to get this job done!

KEY WORDS

train	teach	example
instruct	prayer	godly
knowledge	scriptures	

CHOICES BEFORE US
Either we will fulfill our responsibility or a generation will arise that knows neither God, His ways, the church, nor the Bible.

THREE GREAT TRUTHS
If we fail in this responsibility, we have no one to blame but ourselves.

A child not being prepared for heaven suffers the worst kind of abuse.

Mothers and daddies must stop blaming the church for their failure to teach their own children!

SCRIPTURES TO BE READ AND STUDIED

Proverbs 1:8	Job 8:8; 12:12
Job 22:6; 29:15	Psalm 71:18; 127:3–5
2 Corinthians 12:14	Ephesians 6:1–4
Deuteronomy 6:4–9	Judges 2:10
Ezekiel 16:44	

PRAYER FOR TODAY

Dear God, I need Thy help to teach the children with whom Thou hast blessed me.

Introduction

What shall I teach my child? What a challenging question! Some people take better care of their pets than their children. There are souls at stake and these souls are in our care! In our busy, chaotic, and hell-bound world, we have no time to get the job done! The verses listed above are fading in the sunset! We give our youth everything but God. We have come to believe that things equal love, and that is an eternal tragedy. We give our youth things and then allow them to run with thugs. We have convinced ourselves that we can live like the devil six days a week and fool our children by acting like a saint on Sunday. Not so! It is an awesome responsibility to bring a child into the world. Parenting is a full-time job, and we need help from God, the church, the Bible, and every saint! We owe our children more than room and board. We owe them:

1. A knowledge of the Bible.
2. A godly example.
3. Prayer.
4. An example of dedication and commitment to the church.
5. An example of honesty.
6. The hope of heaven.
7. The Bible's pure view of marriage.
8. An example of marital and parental love.
9. Discipline, including spanking—sometimes an old fashion "whooping."
10. A home where Jesus is always the center of all activity.

What Shall I Teach My Children?

After Solomon had taught his son all he could, he instructed him to go out and make for himself a better world (Prov. 4:10–27). Solomon had done his part; his son was then responsible for personal choices. The following are Solomon's teachings to his son, recorded in the book of Proverbs. Solomon always gives the consequences of the choice his son would make.

Children have the responsibility:

1. To hear, obey, and respect their parents (Prov. 30:17; Matt. 15:4).
2. To choose their friends wisely (Prov. 18:24; 24:21–22; 17:17; 27:10).
3. To choose a mate wisely (Prov. 5:3–4, 11–12; 6:32; Matt. 19:1–9).
4. To obey God (Prov. 1:7; Acts 2:38–47; Rom. 16:16).
5. To guard against temptations (Prov. 7:24–27; James 1:12–15; 1 Cor. 10:13; 2 Pet. 2:9).
6. To control their tongues (Prov. 15:1–4; 18:6–7; James 1:19; 3:1–18).
7. To value a good name (Prov. 22:1; 10:7).
8. To practice self-control (Prov. 16:32; 20:1; 29:3; 2 Pet. 1:6; Acts 24:25; 1 Pet. 2:11; Job 24:15).
9. To learn to work (Prov. 6:6–11; 18:9; 20:4; 24:30–31; 26:16; Rom. 12:11; 2 Thess. 3:10).
10. To study the Bible and allow it to control their minds (Prov. 1:6; 2:6, 11; 2 Tim. 2:15; Rom. 10:17; Ps. 119:128; Eccles. 12:13; Acts 20:32; Gal. 4:30).
11. To respect authority (Prov. 23:22, 26; Rom. 13:1, 7; Matt. 15:4; 1 Pet. 2:17; 5:5; Job 32:6; Ps. 119:6; Tit. 3:1). (This includes proper manners. Saying "yes sir" and "no ma'am," opening doors for girls, and such like.)
12. To know there is but one God-ordained way for salvation (Prov. 13:3; 14:12; Matt. 16:18; Acts 20:28; Eph. 1:22–23; 4:4; Rom. 16:16).
13. To know that things will not satisfy (Prov. 11:28; 23:4; Eccles. 1:14; Zeph. 1:18; 1 Tim. 6:10).
14. To know that they will not always get their way (Prov. 30:15–16; Jonah 4:6–11; Phil. 2:4, 21).

15. To know the seriousness of worshiping God (Prov. 3:9; John 4:23–24; Matt. 6:33; Heb. 10:25).

Conclusion

Any parent can give permission to the children's every request, but it takes courage, conviction, commitment, and real love to say no, and then follow with instruction in the paths of right. We need more parents who will teach their children the choices of life and the consequences of those choices. Parents, please allow your children to know why the church is not in the entertainment business. Please instruct them as to the church's real purpose (Eph. 3:21). Please teach them that we must have Bible authority for all we do. Please teach them that Bible classes are more than drinking Kool-Aid, eating cookies, and planning parties! Teach them about hell, heaven, and the right way to live, dress, talk, and act. If the next generation is to know the ways of God, then we must teach them. Let's be like Abraham who knew how to "command his children and his household after him"! (Gen. 18:19).

QUESTIONS

1. If we fail in this responsibility, we have no one to blame but

   _____.

2. Some people take better care of their pets than they do of their

   _____.

3. We owe our children more than _____ and _____.

4. We have come to believe that _____ equal _____, and that is an eternal _____.

5. We need more _____ who teach their children the choices of _____ and the consequences of each.

6. Parents, please allow your children to know why the _____ is not in the _____ business.

7. Please teach them that we must have _____ for all we do.

8. _____ did his part and then tells his son that he is now _____ for his choices.

9. Please teach them the importance of _____ _____
and that they are more than _____ kool-aid, eating
_____, and planning _____!

10. After Solomon had taught his _____ all he could, he instructed
him to go out and make for himself a better _____.

TRUE OR FALSE

1. ____ According to 1 Kings 1:6, David was pleasing to God as a parent.
2. ____ The Bible can/will control one's mind.
3. ____ We should teach our children to control the tongue.
4. ____ Mothers and daddies must stop blaming the church when they fail to teach their children properly.
5. ____ Second Corinthians 12:14 says children are to lay up for the parents.

FIVE SIMPLE QUESTIONS

1. What scripture in Job challenges us to inquire of the former age?
2. What two verses in Psalms tell us the value of a good name?
3. What verse in Ephesians tells us the purpose of the church?
4. Who is to blame if we fail to teach the next generation?
5. What gets more attention than the children in some households?

46

Plain Bible Talk

ABOUT THE DEVIL

PURPOSE
To study what the Bible says about the origin, mission, and destiny of the devil.

GOAL
To learn more about this evil being and how we can defeat him.

CHALLENGING THOUGHT
If a person does not choose to follow God, the devil will choose him.

KEY WORDS

devil	old serpent	tempter
deceiver	wicked one	god of this world
Satan		

CHOICES BEFORE US
A person will serve either God or Satan; he cannot serve both!

THREE GREAT TRUTHS
Satan was defeated at the cross.
Satan is now trying to defeat Christ's church.
Satan can still be defeated by Christians.

SCRIPTURES TO BE READ AND STUDIED
John 8:44; 12:31   Genesis 1:31
2 Peter 2:4   Jude 6
Matthew 4:1–11   Matthew 25:31–46
James 4:7   1 Peter 5:8

PRAYER FOR TODAY
Dear God, we beg Thee to give us wisdom and courage to defeat the devil.

Introduction

1. The devil is real (John 8:44).
2. He is either (1) a god co-equal with Jehovah God or (2) a created evil being, or (3) a created angel who chose to rebel against God. Considering Genesis 1:31; 2 Peter 2:4; and Jude 6, the latter seems to be the proper answer.
3. His mission is to prohibit souls from going to heaven (Matt. 25:31–46; Rev. 12:13–17).
4. His destiny is eternal hell (Matt. 25:31–46; Rev. 20:11–15).
5. He has preachers (2 Cor. 11:14–15).
6. He has followers (John 6:70; Rev. 20:11–15).
7. He sometimes quotes scripture but misuses and abuses it (Matt. 4:6).
8. He has been overcome by our Lord (John 12:31; 16:11; Rev. 12:1–12).
9. He can still be resisted and defeated by Christians because of our Lord's work (Rev. 12:13–17; James 4:7).
10. He is our adversary (1 Pet. 5:8).
11. He is the prince of this world (John 12:31).
12. He cannot stand it when scriptures are quoted and properly applied (Matt. 4:1–11; Eph. 6:10–11).
13. Do not give in to him (Eph. 4:27).
14. Some names by which the Bible calls him: devil, Satan, tempter, liar, prince of this world, deceiver, god of this world, old serpent, roaring lion, murderer, wicked one, and Beelzebub.

15. Five ways we can defeat him and cause all the demons in hell to fear: live a pure life, win a soul, stand for truth, be happy, and be faithful in service and worship to God!

How Can We Bring Satan's Kingdom Down?

In Trinidad's mission fields, we used to sing, "Satan, Your Kingdom Must Come Down." What a beautiful thought and lesson! The following six points are the gist of that challenging song. Oh, how I hate Satan and all his ways! Every day he snatches souls from eternal bliss. He is crafty and wily. It is my prayer that all of us will do our part to bring Satan's kingdom down!

1. "I will sing and bring his kingdom down" (Eph. 5:19). A psalm is praise to God. A hymn is a song of thanksgiving and dependence upon God. A spiritual song is one that brings one's spirit under God's control. No wonder singing helps to bring Satan's kingdom down! Songs like "Sing and Be Happy" makes Satan's knees knock! As Christians, we are to be happy because God rules and all is well! When we sing, let's take note of the words and consider what we are saying. Satan cannot stand a sincere, singing Christian.

2. "I will pray and bring his kingdom down" (Matt. 21:22; Heb. 4:16; Hab. 2:20). When we pray to God in the name of Christ and according to His will, we are beating old Satan into submission! When one carries his burdens, heartaches, and troubles before God's throne, the devil knows he is in a peck of trouble with that person. Songs like "Sweet Hour of Prayer" are powerful stuff against Satan's kingdom. Always remember that worry is a prayer to the wrong god!

3. "I will preach and bring his kingdom down" (2 Tim. 4:2). When a man preaches what God said, Satan shudders! That is how Jesus handled Satan (Matt. 4:1–11). If we had more men preaching God's message, Satan's kingdom would be on the run. Satan cannot cross the bloodline; real Bible preaching emphasizes that. Let's sing more songs like "Give Me the Bible." All the world must hear what God said (Jer. 22:29), and this will cause Satan's kingdom to come down!

4. "I will work and bring his kingdom down" (1 John 3:18; Tit. 3:1; 1 Cor. 15:58; John 9:4). Songs like "I Want to Be a Worker for the

Lord" are very challenging. Apathy and idleness are Satan's chief weapons. "Shall your brethren go to war while you sit here?" (Num. 32:7). The church is worth fighting and working for! Working in God's kingdom will help bring down Satan's kingdom.

5. "I will teach and bring his kingdom down" (Heb. 5:12; 2 Tim. 2:2, 15). When we sing "Send the Light," we are emphasizing the importance of teaching. One cannot teach what he does not know, So we should study and prepare to teach others. Pulpit preaching alone will not prepare you for this privilege and responsibility. To Satan, teaching others the Bible is like light to a vampire. Every funeral is a reminder of the importance of teaching lost souls. Is it not now time for many to teach instead of being taught? Read Matthew 28:18–20.

6. "I will baptize and bring his kingdom down" (Luke 7:30; Acts 2:38–47). Many reject baptism and therefore reject the counsel of God! "Trust and Obey" is a beautiful song. Baptism not only puts one into Christ (Gal. 3:26–27), but it also displays great faith in the risen Savior! (Mark 16:16). Baptism allows one to contact the blood of Christ (Acts 22;16; Rev. 1:5). That is why I will continue to emphasize baptism. What about you?

Satan, your kingdom must come down!

QUESTIONS

1. Satan was defeated at the _____.
2. Satan's mission is to _____ souls from going to _____.
3. Satan's destiny is eternal _____.
4. Each and every day, he snatches _____ from eternal _____.
5. As Christians, we are to be _____ because God _____ and all is well!
6. Always remember that _____ is a prayer to the wrong god!
7. When a man preaches what God said, Satan _____!
8. _____ and _____ are chief weapons of Satan.
9. Every _____ is a reminder of the importance of teaching lost _____.
10. Many reject baptism, and therefore reject the _____ of God!

TRUE OR FALSE

1. ____ Satan is co-equal with God.
2. ____ Satan never quotes scripture.
3. ____ Satan is called the prince of this world.
4. ____ Satan was defeated by the cross of Calvary.
5. ____ Satan will choose you if you do not choose to follow God.

FIVE SIMPLE QUESTIONS

1. Name five ways Satan can be defeated.
2. List eleven other names the Bible uses for Satan.
3. What scripture tells us to resist Satan?
4. What two scriptures teach that upon being baptized, a person is washed in the blood of Jesus?
5. What scripture calls Satan our adversary?

47

Plain Bible Talk

ABOUT THE
TEN COMMANDMENTS

PURPOSE
To learn more about the Ten Commandments found in Exodus 20:1–17.

GOAL
To see why these commandments are the very foundation upon which the law of Moses was based.

CHALLENGING THOUGHT
For any of these commandments to be valid today, they must be incorporated into the New Testament.

KEY WORDS
Exodus	Jews	commandments
law	God	fulfilled
Gentiles	justify	sins

CHOICES BEFORE US
Either the old law was nailed to the cross, or God lied and it is still valid as a standard of worship and living.

THREE GREAT TRUTHS
The Ten Commandments were given to the Israelites.

They were taken out of the way and nailed to the cross.

We now have a better law.

SCRIPTURES TO BE READ AND STUDIED

Romans 2:14	Galatians 1:13
Ezekiel 20:10–12	Nehemiah 9:13–14
Exodus 31:16	Deuteronomy 5:1–6
John 10:33–34	John 8:17; 15:25
Colossians 2:14	Romans 7:6
Hebrews 7:22; 8:7	

PRAYER FOR TODAY
Dear God, please help us to rightly divide Thy word.

Introduction

The Ten Commandments can be divided into two groups: (1) The first four are responsibilities toward God; (2) the next six are commands of duties toward mankind. Jesus gives an example of this in Matthew 22:34–40. Again, these ten are the foundation on which the whole law is based. There are 613 laws found in the law of Moses.

1. We are no longer under the law of Moses (Col. 2:14; Rom. 7:6; Heb. 8:6–7; 10:9).
2. It is no longer needed (Gal. 3:24–25; Acts 13:29).
3. Attempting to keep it today will cause one to fall from grace (Gal. 5:4).
4. If it is valid today, Christ died in vain (Gal. 2:21).
5. It justifies no one (Gal. 3:11).
6. It did not solve man's sin problem (Heb. 10:4).
7. Everyone since Pentecost is under the new law (Acts 2:38–47).

Of What Value Are the Ten Commandments?

Paul's assertion that the "things written aforetime were written for our learning" (Rom. 15:4), and the fact that the principles of these commandments are found in the New Testament make them worthy of our study (Exodus 20:1–17). Consider the Ten Commandments:

1. Verse 3: *"Thou shalt have no other gods before me."* This commandment is the very foundation upon which everything else rests. Without it, there is no standard of right and wrong. Read Exodus 34:14;

Isaiah 45:5; Matthew 22:37; and Ephesians 4:6. Lesson: There is only one true God!

2. Verse 4: "*Thou shalt not make unto thee any graven image, or any likeness of any thing that is in heaven above, or that is in the earth beneath, or that is in the water under the earth.*" No person, place, or thing is to be put ahead of God, else it becomes idolatry. Whatever we value more than we value God becomes our "golden calf" (Exod. 32:4–6). Lesson: We must not love anything or anyone more than we love God (Matt. 22:37–38; 1 John 5:21).

3. Verse 7: "*Thou shalt not take the name of the Lord thy God in vain, for the Lord will not hold him guiltless that taketh his name in vain.*" *Vain* means to waste. It is wrong to waste God's holy name (Ps. 111:9). Never use His name lightly, jokingly, or wastefully. We can be guilty of doing so by singing unscriptural songs as well. Lesson: There is most certainly something in a name—especially in God's name!

4. Verse 8: "*Remember the Sabbath day, to keep it holy.*" The Israelites understood this to mean every Sabbath! The specified day to worship God was the seventh day, Saturday. We also have a specified day—Sunday, the first day of the week (Acts 20:7). Lesson: Do not forsake the assembly (Heb. 10:25). We have an appointment with God.

5. Verse 12: "*Honor thy father and thy mother: that thy days may be long upon the land which the Lord thy God giveth thee.*" The welfare of society has always depended upon submission to authority, and submission begins in the home. This is certainly true of today (Eph. 6:1–4). Lesson: Honor your parents at home, school, work, and play.

6. Verse 13: "*Thou shalt not kill.*" Literally: Thou shalt do no murder. Abortion is murder. Lesson: Yes, murder is wrong and even hate is classified as murder (Rev. 21:8; 1 John 3:15).

7. Verse 14: "*Thou shalt not commit adultery.*" What a plague adultery has been in the world! Marriage is a sacred, life-long relationship (Gen. 2:18–24; Prov. 6:32; Matt. 19:1–9). Adultery is the fruit of selfishness and fleshly appetite. Lesson: Adultery is sin, a destroyer of the home.

8. Verse 15: *"Thou shalt not steal."* This includes robbing God and man (Mal. 1:7–12; Eph. 4:28). Robbing another of his material things, wife, name, or character is wrong. Even gambling is robbery by consent. Lesson: It is sin to take anything that belongs to another.

9. Verse 16: *"Thou shalt not bear false witness against thy neighbor."* This must be a way of life, not just for a court room! Slander, half-truths, lies, misquotes, and false flattery are included in this. Speaking the truth is God's way (Eph. 4:25). Lesson: This commandment is a protection against slander.

10. Verse 17: *"Thou shalt not covet thy neighbor's house, thou shalt not covet thy neighbor's wife, nor his manservant, nor his maidservant, nor his ox, nor his ass, nor anything that is thy neighbor's."* Others' possessions do not belong to us, and we should be content with our "stuff." (Luke 12:15; 1 Tim. 6:8; Col. 3:5; Heb. 13:5). Both rich and poor are guilty of being covetous. Lesson: People—especially their souls—are important, not things.

Questions

1. For these commandments to be _____ today, they must be _____ (or restated) into the New Testament

2. The _____ commandments were given to the _____.

3. Keeping it (old law) today, will cause one to _____ from grace.

4. They were taken out of the way and _____ to the cross.

5. Again, these 10 are the _____ on which the whole law is based.

6. There are some _____ laws found in the law of Moses.

7. We now have a better _____.

8. If it (old law) is valid today, _____ died in vain.

9. The old law remitted sins. Yes or no? _____

10. What scripture in Galatians states the old law justified no one? _____

True or False

1. _____ Exodus 20:3 proves one can choose what god he wants to serve.

2. _____ The word *vain* means to waste.

3. _____ God commands us to keep the Sabbath day.

4. _____ In the commandment, "Thou shalt not kill," *kill* literally means murder.

5. _____ "Thou shalt not bear false witness against thy neighbor" regulates conduct only in a court of law.

Five Simple Questions

1. What scripture in Psalms tells us God's name is holy?

2. What scripture in Acts tells us that the first-century church partook of the Lord's supper on the first day of the week?

3. What scriptures in Matthew tell us that adultery is the only reason for the divorce and remarriage of an innocent mate?

4. What scriptures in Malachi tell us that the Jews were guilty of robbing God?

5. What scripture in 1 John tells us that hating our brother is the same as murder?

48

Plain Bible Talk

ABOUT RESPONSIBILITY AND EXCUSE-MAKING

PURPOSE
To begin taking responsibility for our choices and stop offering excuses.

GOAL
To learn that we cannot blame someone else, or something else, for our wrong choices.

CHALLENGING THOUGHT
Saying "it really ain't my fault" is a sign of immaturity, irresponsibility, excuse making, and blaming others for your choices and sin.

KEY WORDS

excuses	choices	responsibility
self-pity	immature	whine
complain		

CHOICES BEFORE US
Either we will submit to the teachings of the Bible and take responsibility for our actions, or we will find a "crutch" and blame others for the choices we make.

THREE GREAT TRUTHS
The devil cannot make anyone do anything.
I must take responsibility for my choices.
No one is born with a gene that makes him sin!

SCRIPTURES TO BE READ AND STUDIED

Genesis 3:11–12; 43:9	Exodus 32:24
Deuteronomy 24:16	1 Kings 12:28
Ecclesiastes 7:29	Luke 14:18
John 15:22	Romans 1:20
Romans 14:12	2 Corinthians 5:10

PRAYER FOR TODAY

*Dear God, give me the courage to admit my mistakes
and assume responsibility for my bad choices.*

Introduction

We live in a society that is engulfed with self-pity, selfishness, and people who have mastered the ploy of blaming others for bad and sinful choices. Most folks no longer take responsibility for personal choices. When a person sins or is found in a bad situation, he usually begins the "blame game." He immediately says that parental influence, society, environment, or some wild genetic trait "made me do this." It is common to hear blame placed on someone else or something else. It may be a "fat" gene, a mind-altering drug, murder, alcohol, fornication, adultery, pedophilia, theft, abortion, spousal abuse, tobacco, or even telling children they have ADD (Attention Deficit Disorder).

Is anyone at fault anymore? Liberals blame the church for being too strict. Children blame their evil deeds and drug usage on their parents. Many blame their surroundings for being sinners. Many take the self-pity route and whine to high heaven. The immoral blame parents for passing down a gene that causes them to fornicate, take drugs, shoplift, drink alcohol, and overspend. The unfaithful blame the church, preacher, elders, or a fellow member. The man outside Christ often blames the church of Christ for teaching a strict adherence to the Bible.

Read Luke 14:15–24 and notice this statement: "They all with one consent began to make excuse" (v. 18). This is a summation of our study today. Let's look at some excuses folks give for not being members of the church of Christ or for not being faithful. Peter told those in Acts 2 that they, not others, were responsible for their sin (Acts 2:22, 23, 37–38, 41, 47).

1. *"I do not like the preacher."* Does he preach the truth? What has he said that offends you? Why do you not like him? He likes you. You and I can go and talk with him about it, or I'm sure he will gladly come to your house. Do you really know him? One must worship God and not the preacher.

2. *"No one ever visits me."* I am here. Would you like others to visit you? I can have fifty here by tonight. Would this bring you back to church? Do you ever visit others?

3. *"There are hypocrites at church."* If someone gave you a counterfeit twenty dollar bill, would you stop taking twenty dollar bills? Don't use hypocrisy as an excuse. Judas was among the apostles. He walked daily with Jesus for more than three years. Tell me who the hypocrites are at church and you and I can go visit them. Then you can think of all the good folks at church. We do not claim perfection as Christians, but we do strive to be faithful.

4. *"My job demands all my spare time."* Have you ever read the story of the rich man in Luke 12? God called him a fool. Has God not promised to provide, protect, and shelter us? (Matt. 6:19–34).

5. *"Sunday is the only day I have to spend with my family and/or enjoy recreation."* Whose day is it, yours or the Lord's? Please consider what Jesus went through on the cross in order that we could worship God on Sunday. Read Matthew 6:33 and Mark 4:19. Have you stopped loving the Lord?

6. *"One of the members offended me one time and I just cannot attend anymore."* Let's go see him right now. It may be just a misunderstanding or an oversight on his part. If that is the only thing preventing you from being faithful, we can resolve it immediately. Read Matthew 18:15–17.

7. *"The church is just too strict and too narrow minded."* Tell me what teaching is too narrow minded or too strict. You can be assured that I will speak with the elders about this, and if we are guilty, we will change. Will you be at the next service if I do this? Read Revelation 22:18–19.

8. *"I have studied my way out of your way of thinking."* We teach only what the Bible authorizes. Please tell me what teaching you no longer

believe to be right. What made us to differ? We both cannot be right, but we both can be wrong. Let's open the Bible and discuss it. Will you allow the Bible to provide the final answers to our questions?

9. *"If you all will wait until I straighten out my life and problems, I will be back."* The church is a place for people with problems and we can help you solve them. Please do not wait until you are straightened out in a casket for the church's help. Read Luke 16:19–31.

10. *"My family and I have been mistreated at church."* How have you been mistreated? Has the church as a whole mistreated you? If some individual has mistreated you, why take it out on the Lord and His church? Is the problem big enough to cause you to lose your soul? Have you discussed this with those who have mistreated you? I will visit them with you and try to help resolve the problem.

11. *"My children do not like attending there. They are condemned for doing certain things. Besides that, you don't have children's church."* Have your children quit school because they did not like it? Was the truth taught concerning what your children were guilty of? Do you realize that there is absolutely no biblical authority for children's church? Read Colossians 3:17.

12. *"God has turned His back on me."* Do you really believe that? In what way has God turned His back on you? Is this just an excuse? Let's talk about it. Read 1 Peter 5:7 and Hebrews 13:5.

QUESTIONS

1. I must take _____ for the choices I make.
2. No one is born with a _____ that makes him sin!
3. We live in a society that is engulfed with _____ _____, _____, and people that have mastered the ploy of _____ others for bad and sinful _____.
4. _____ blame the church for being too _____.
5. The _____ blames the church, preacher, elders, or some other _____.
6. The _____ cannot "make" anyone do anything.
7. "They all with one _____ began to make _____."

8. Has God not promised to _____, _____, and shelter us?
9. One must worship God, and not the _____.
10. Please do not wait until you are "_____ _____" in a casket and then want the _____ help.

TRUE OR FALSE

1. ____ The adulterer is born with a gene that makes him commit that sin.
2. ____ Peter told the Jews on Pentecost that the crucifixion of Christ was not their fault.
3. ____ According to 2 Corinthians 5:10, each person will answer for his own sins.
4. ____ God called the rich man in Luke 12 a fool.
5. ____ Hebrews 13:5 says God will forsake us.

FIVE SIMPLE QUESTIONS

1. What book, chapter, and verses tell the story of the rich man and Lazarus?
2. What chapter and verses in Matthew teach us to go to the one who sinned against us?
3. Although Christians are not perfect, what is the goal for which we should strive?
4. Why should a Christian take his problems to the church?
5. What verse in 1 Peter tells us to cast our care upon God because He cares for us?

49

Plain Bible Talk

ABOUT MAKING OUR HOME A CHRISTIAN HOME

PURPOSE
To learn the role of each family member in making a Christian home.

GOAL
For each member—father, mother, child—to learn and accept his or her role.

CHALLENGING THOUGHT
I wish I had been taught this lesson when I was young and before I was married.

KEY WORDS

house	home	God
mother	daddy	children
Bible	church	rules
discipline		

CHOICES BEFORE US
Christians make a house either a Christian home or just a material structure.

THREE GREAT LESSONS
Daddy must be the head of the home.
We need mother back in the home.
We must not allow children to take over the home.

SCRIPTURES TO BE READ AND STUDIED

Genesis 2:18–25	2 Kings 20:15
Proverbs 22:6	Ephesians 6:1–4
Colossians 3:21	Titus 2:2–5
Proverbs 17:6	Psalm 71:18; 92:12–14
Matthew 15:4	Ecclesiastes 11:8–9; 12:1

PRAYER FOR TODAY

Dear God, help us to love each other and turn our house into a home.

Introduction

"What have they seen in your house?" (2 Kings 20:15). This is a challenging and thought-provoking question to every husband, wife, father, and mother! The home as God would have it is fading in the sunset in many places. We urgently need to pass down to the next generation the truths of what constitutes a Christian home. Neither a castle nor a run-down shack is necessarily a home!

A Home Is a Place Where . . .

1. Parents are faithful Christians and make every effort to teach their children God's ways.
2. There is a little bit of heaven on earth. The key is Matthew 6:33.
3. The Word of God and the church are always put first.
4. Love and joy are found, and sharing is a way of life.
5. The Bible is read, and a foundation for all decisions is laid.
6. Daddy is the head, Mother can be found, and children have not taken over.
7. Each member takes responsibility and makes an efforts to keep pure the family name.
8. Fun, laughter, and good, wholesome entertainment are healthy ingredients.
9. Rules are determined by the Bible and discipline is practiced.
10. A man and woman live together with their children, if any, in accordance with the Scriptures.

11. The family stands together for the right and against the wrong.

12. God is the ever-present guest and Satan is never welcome.

13. The members make God proud and contribute to the integrity of the local congregation.

14. Mother, Daddy, and children exalt God's name together (Ps. 34:3).

15. Daddy really loves Mother, Mother really loves Daddy, both love the children, children love the parents, and all family members express their love in word and in deed.

God's Arrangement for a Christian Home

1. *The man as father, husband, and spiritual leader.* So are we mice or men? If we would fulfill our God-given roles, many of the problems of the home would be resolved! The wife and children deserve a Christian leader. That is more than providing material things. It involves spiritual teaching, training, leadership, and example (2 Cor. 12:14, Eph. 5:25). No woman wants a hen-pecked, wimpy, wishy-washy husband. Neither do the children need to see those characteristics in Daddy.

   Yes, he should provide necessary material things, too. For the man of the house to be respected, he must be respectful! So a man should love his wife and treat her as the queen and the first lady of his life. Be kind, courteous, polite, gentle, affectionate, understanding, patient, sweet, and thankful for all she does. Court her, buy her gifts, walk proudly by her side, hold her hand, take her out on a "date," vacuum, wash dishes, clean up after yourself, open doors for her, carry the baby, help tend to your children at home and at church, wash her back, polish her nails, and kill spiders, snakes, and bugs for her. A real man will honor, praise, and be faithful to his wife!

   Be a real daddy and an example for your children. Assume responsibility: teach them respect, manners, and obedience to God. Pray for them, praise them, spend time with them, and help them get to heaven. Be their daddy and not just their pal! Be loving yet firm. Act like a real man, not a wimp!

2. *The woman as mother, wife, and supporter.* Ladies, are you real or just pretending? Every facet of society is begging for real Christian

wives and mothers! Be a Christian and a real lady in speech, dress, demeanor, and attitude. Take pride in being a woman. In our materialistic, hell-bound, and self-centered world, we need Christian ladies! A Christian mother does not scream, yell, and act like a wildcat! She is feminine and loves her family. She reveres, honors, compliments, loves, supports, and encourages her husband. She does not flirt or have bedroom eyes for other men. She allows her husband to be her protector. She treats him as her king, the first gentleman in her life. She is sweet, kind, tender, considerate, and compassionate. She holds his hand and makes his favorite pie. She puts love notes in his lunch box or shirt pocket. She takes time to be the mother of his children and the grandmother of his grandchildren. She helps him on his way to heaven.

Be a real mother and an example for your children. Love them and teach them about God, the church, Christ, and the Bible. Teach them about life and how to guard against the evils that abound. Help them get to heaven. Accept the role as queen of your domain.

3. *Young people, have you taken over the home, or are you trying to?* Your responsibility in the home is not to make the rules! The church has bombarded you with youth rallies, lock-ins, retreats, fireside chats, entertainment, hot dogs, chips, dip, ice cream, and whatever appeals to the flesh. We have coddled, petted, spoiled, pampered, and compromised the truth in order to please you and keep you coming to church. This has been a mistake because we owe you the truth so you can develop into a mature Christian and eventually get to heaven. We love you, but we have forsaken our responsibility to teach you about Bible characters, books, and subjects. For this we are sorry! All the youth rallies in the world will not replace basic, fundamental truths about marriage, baptism, and the one church, or provide instructions on how to live, dress, and act. They will not indelibly imprint truths about the dangers of drinking alcohol, smoking tobacco, fornicating, and shooting dope. They will not do these things because they cannot. Training for service in Christ must be administered constantly, not given in capsules of brief, emotional high points.

Young people, life is filled with winners and losers, Accept responsibility for your actions. Just remember this: When you are done with sin, it is not done with you.

Be a real Christian young person. Be polite and well-mannered. Respect your parents, the Bible, and all in authority. Love and admire older Christians. Learn that you will not always get your way. You think being young is hard? Wait until you became a parent who is trying to raise a young person in the ways of the Lord!

QUESTIONS

1. Christians make a _____ either a Christian _____ or just a material _____.

2. Neither a _____ nor a run-down _____ is necessarily a home!

3. A Christian home is where the _____ of _____ and the church are always put _____.

4. A Christian home is where _____, _____, and children exalt God's _____ together.

5. A Christian home is where the _____ is read and is the source of all _____ made.

6. A Christian home is where the _____ stands together for the _____ and against the _____.

7. A Christian home is where there is a little _____ of _____ on earth.

8. A Christian home is where _____ is the ever present guest and _____ is never welcome.

9. A Christian home is where _____ and _____ are found, and where the word _____ is a way of life.

10. A Christian home is where _____ is the head, _____ can be found, and _____ have not taken over.

TRUE OR FALSE

1. ____ According to 2 Corinthians 12:14, children are to lay up for the parents.

2. ____ Husbands and wives should help each other get to heaven.
3. ____ There are no consequences to sin, because when you are through with sin, it is through with you.
4. ____ God has given the man the responsibility of being the spiritual leader of the home.
5. ____ We should just teach our children the right ways and not train them.

FIVE SIMPLE QUESTIONS

1. What verses in the book of Psalms declare children as a heritage of the Lord?
2. What verse in the book of Proverbs teaches parents to train their children?
3. What verses in the book of Ephesians command children to obey their parents in the Lord?
4. What verses in the book of Ecclesiastes state that young people can do what they wish, but God will bring them into judgment?
5. What verse in the book of Ephesians teaches fathers not to provoke their children to wrath?

50

Plain Bible Talk

ABOUT CEMETERIES, GRAVES, AND TOMBSTONES

Purpose
To study about dying and being prepared for the time of departure.

Goal
To realize that there are no changes after death.

Challenging Thought
The only thing that truly matters is to die in the Lord.

Key Words

death	judgment	grave
body	soul	eternity
heaven	hell	cemetery

Choices Before Us
Every death is a reminder that a soul is either prepared or unprepared to meet God; there is no "in between."

Three Great Lessons
All must die.
All will be raised.
All will be judged.

Scriptures to Be Read and Studied

Gen. 5:5, 8, 11, 14, 17	Gen. 5:20, 24, 25, 31; 27:2
1 Samuel 20:3	Hebrews 9:27; 11:4
Revelation 14:13	Job 10:19
2 Corinthians 5:10	1 Kings 2:11
Ecclesiastes 9:10	Luke 16:26

Prayer for Today

Dear God, please help me to prepare to pass over the chilly waters.

General Observations

1. We are obligated to teach our children about death; that it is a part of the life cycle. Young people should be exposed to funerals, cemeteries, and other things associated with death. Those things teach them a lot about life.

2. Death, funerals, cemeteries, and graves are part of the Bible (Gen. 35:20; Deut. 34:7–8; Matt. 23:29; 1 Cor. 15:50–58).

3. Cemeteries can usually be recognized (Luke 11:44).

4. Cemeteries are reminders that we must prepare for eternity (Amos 4:12).

5. Cemeteries teach us there are no changes after death (Luke 16:26).

6 Death is precious to the saint (Ps. 116:15), but the funeral of the unprepared is sad (Eccles. 8:10). Yes, some funerals are sadder than others! (1 Thess. 4:13).

7. One cannot live one kind of life and die another (2 Cor. 5:10).

8. One day there will be no more need for cemeteries, graves, and tombstones (John 5:28–29).

Nine Lessons from Cemeteries, Graves, and Tombstones

A visit to the cemetery might cause sadness or joy, but it can teach some challenging lessons. The following examples are about folks whom I have known whose bodies lie in a nearby cemetery. Walk with me through this burial place and look at nine tombstones. Note each example, and then determine how you stand with the Lord (Acts 2:38; Rev. 2:10).

1. We come to the grave of a man who lived some seventy years, "and he died." He attended a few church services, had an abundance of material possessions, was successful in business, and had friends. Yet he was a self-proclaimed atheist. He told me so as I tried to teach him the Bible. He rejected God and went to his grave as a fool (Ps. 14:1). Lesson: Do not die a fool! Read Daniel 2:28.

2. Near the atheist's grave is the tombstone of a baby. I knew this baby personally. He was precious, sweet, and beautiful! He came into this world with severe health problems and lived two months, "and he died." At the time of his death, his parents were faithful members of the church of Christ. He is now in the "arms of Jesus" (Luke 18:15–17). Lesson: All babies will be in heaven and parents can be with them if they remain faithful (Rev. 2:10).

3. Here lies the body of a successful businessman, a wealthy and decent neighbor. But he was not a friendly person and was rarely nice to children. He was a worldly man, "and he died." Lesson: Loving the world will rob you of your soul (1 John 2:15–17).

4. Here is another tombstone that marks the grave of a young Christian girl. She was but a teenager, "and she died." She was a beautiful, sweet, and likeable person. She and her family were very close friends of ours. One Friday night a drunken driver hit her car head on. Thankfully, she had sought God in her youth (Eccl. 12:1). Lesson: Death plays no favorites so cemeteries are full of young people. Read Ecclesiastes 11:8–9.

5. We now see the grave of an elderly woman. She served God faithfully in her younger years but turned away later in life, "and she died." She was not a mean person; she simply stopped loving God. After she became unfaithful, her husband, son, and daughter did likewise. Read 2 Peter 2:20–22. Lesson: For some people, it would have been good never to have been born (Mark 14:21).

6. Next we come upon a husband and wife. This married couple had no time for God. They had three children and were not very old when they left this earth, "and they died." They were party goers. They frequented honky-tonks, fought, fussed, and had little trust it each

other. The cares of the world had a hold on them (Mark 4:19). Lesson: Those who do not heed to the teaching of the judgment, exercise self-control, or engage in righteous living have no promise of eternal life (Acts 24:25).

7. We now find the tombstone of a family of religious people. They were well known and respected in town. They were helpful to others, an asset to the community and to the local school. But they had no room for truth and the one church for which our Lord died (Matt. 15:8–9; 16:18). Their church was started by man. They were religious but religiously wrong, "and they died." Lesson: One must obey God rather than man (Acts 5:29).

8. We walk to the grave of a Christian lady. For several years, she had forsaken God and His ways and enjoyed the pleasures of the world. But she repented and "came back home." Read Acts 8:22–24. She was faithful to God the last several years she lived, "and she died." Lesson: The only thing that really matters is dying in the Lord (Rev. 14:13).

9. The last grave we see is that of a Christian lady who served God over seventy-five years, "and she died." She never had a lot of material things, her husband was a drunk, she had no home of her own, and three of her children died when they were babies. Yet this godly woman never wavered, and she encouraged many to become Christians and remain faithful. Lesson: To hear Jesus say "Well done good and faithful servant" says it all! (Matt. 25:21).

QUESTIONS

1. Every death is a reminder that a _____ is either prepared or _____ to meet God. There is no "____ _____."

2. All must _____. All will be _____. All will be _____.

3. _____ can usually be recognized.

4. One cannot _____ one kind of life and _____ another.

5. One day, there will be no more need for _____, _____, and _____.

6. The only thing that truly matters is to _____ in the _____.
7. Yes, some _____ are more sad than others.
8. A visit to the _____ will cause sadness or _____, but can also teach some challenging _____.
9. Cemeteries are reminders that we must prepare for _____.
10. Death is _____ to the saint, but the funeral of the unprepared is _____.

TRUE OR FALSE

1. ____ God says the man who denies Him is a wise man.
2. ____ Loving the world will rob a person's soul.
3. ____ According to Ecclesiastes 11:8–9, young people will not face God in the judgment.
4. ____ According to 2 Peter 2:20–22, a person can turn away from God and be lost.
5. ____ One must be faithful unto death in order to receive the crown of life.

FIVE SIMPLE QUESTIONS

1. What verse teaches that one must obey God rather than man?
2. What verse teaches that a person will answer to God for the things done in the body, whether good or bad?
3. What verse challenges everyone to "prepare to meet thy God"?
4. Name the verse that states it would have been better if Judas had never been born.
5. Will all babies be in heaven? Why or why not?

51

ABOUT GLUTTONY

PURPOSE
To discuss the "forgotten and ignored" sin of gluttony.

GOAL
To reveal how harmful and sinful gluttony really is.

CHALLENGING THOUGHT
When is the last time you heard a lesson or a sermon on gluttony? When have you studied it for yourself?

KEY WORDS

obese	excess	self-control
crave	fast	health
ruin	desire	abuse

CHOICES BEFORE US
Either the Bible is right and gluttony is a sin, or society has "outgrown" this sin and the Bible is out of date.

THREE GREAT LESSONS
Gluttony is a sin; it shows a lack of self-control.

It is not wrong to have some weight on the bones; a person does not have to look like a stick.

It not only matters what but also how much a person puts into his body.

Matthew 11:19	Titus 1:12
Habakkuk 2:10	Proverbs 23:20–21; 25:16
3 John 21	1 Corinthians 6:19–20
2 Peter 2:19	Romans 12:1–2; 14:21
Daniel 1:8	Judges 3:17

Prayer for Today

Dear God, help me to practice self-control in all things.

Introduction

One can be a glutton in ways other than overeating, but the lesson today deals with the basic meaning of the word: "to overeat, hoggish, to eat too much, a belly, excessive love of food, excessive indulgence." The Bible makes clear and plain the sin of gluttony (Matt. 11:19; Prov. 23:20–21). Do you want to see what God thinks of a glutton? Then read Deuteronomy 21:18–21! Let's get right to the point. There is no polite, politically correct, or weasel way to say it. Eating too much is a sin! (Gal. 4:16, 30).

Several years ago, the author preached a sermon on gluttony. One very large and overweight man took exception to the sermon. He soon thereafter told a friend of mine that I should be taken behind the church building and given a good whipping, and he said he was the man to do it. Instead of realizing that this lesson is designed to help and save souls, some become upset. I pray that the guilty one will heed the warning and repent.

Early Christians were alarmed and concerned about gluttony. Today it is seldom mentioned, and most certainly is not preached about. Gluttony has become one of the accepted sins of our time. To abstain from gluttony, one must practice self-control, and herein lies the problem. Self-control is no longer in our vocabulary!

According to Edward Gibbon, three of the seven reasons for Rome's fall were gluttony, drunkenness, and immorality. Rome provided designated vomiting rooms at feasts. After expelling their food, the feasters returned to the table to continue their enjoyment. We have added all kinds of slimming diets and pills to the ancient vomiting rooms. We, like Rome, encourage bulimia.

Sin is a perversion of what is good, an abuse of the wholesome, and a misuse of the natural. Gluttony fits that description; it is a sin! We should enjoy food and drink and thank God for them, but we must be temperate and exercise self-control. Brethren, let's face it. We have a big problem in our fat and self-indulgent society. We are like the folks in the days of Amos (4:1, 4–6). We crave comfort and bodily pleasures! God looks upon those who squander their stewardship as gluttons. The prodigal son is an example (Luke 15:11–32). Paul told the Corinthians to be temperate in all things (1 Cor. 9:25–27). In our mad rush for wealth, things, and satisfying the body, the soul is forgotten (Mark 8:36–37).

Do We Eat to Live or Live to Eat?

Titus 1:12 states that some in Paul's day were "dull, heavy, and lazy." Sound familiar?

1. Gluttony is the inordinate desire of the sense of taste.
2. Overeating is a basic definition of gluttony. Yes, a slim person can be guilty of gluttony also!
3. To ask, "Well, just how much is too much?" is like asking how long is a man's hair when it's too long, or how short is a woman's skirt when it's too short? God gives us scripture (Tit. 1:12; 1 Cor. 11:14; 1 Tim. 2:9) and sense enough to know! If I offered a man a million dollars not to have long hair or a woman a million dollars to dress modestly, could that person determine the limits? I think so! What if I offered you a million dollars not to overeat? You would have no problem defining the boundaries and exercising self-control.
4. Gluttony is the undue desire of, or affection to, the pleasures of the palate.
5. Gluttony is to eat to the excess, to lavish, or to squander or waste.
6. Gluttony is to set up your belly as a god (Phil. 3:18–19; Prov. 25:16).
7. Gluttony was one of the fundamental practices of the Epicureans: "enjoy thyself" (Acts 17).
8. The opposite virtue of gluttony is temperance (self-control).

9. Even though fasting—which means "cover the mouth"—is not a command of God, we would do well to practice it (Acts 13:2–3; 1 Cor. 7:5). *Breakfast* means to break your fast.

10. The application of 1 Corinthians 10:31 is sorely needed today.

Gluttony Harms and Destroys the Body

1. Gluttony will shorten the lifespan, and that is a fact! It is an epidemic!

2. Three hundred thousand people per year die of gluttony—obesity is too much body fat.

3. The preacher who is guilty of gluttony cannot point a finger at the smoker, drunkard, or drug user. The fat, lazy preacher must bring himself under control (1 Tim. 4:12; 2 Pet. 1:5–11).

4. Sixty-one percent of adults in the U.S. are overweight (gluttonous, obese). Forty-three percent of young people who watch television, play video games, or stay on the computer two hours a day are obese.

5. Those guilty of gluttony and a lack of exercise have a 50 to 100 percent increased risk of premature death. Just as some smokers do not die an early death, neither do some gluttons. These are exceptions!

6. Overweight young people become 70 percent of the obese adults. One-third of young people between the ages of 12 and 19 are obese or on the verge of being so. If one parent is obese, there is an 80 percent chance that the children will be also.

7. Gluttony—which causes obesity, which causes overweight people—causes type 2 diabetes, heart disease, high blood pressure, some forms of cancer, abnormal heart rhythm, arthritis, depression, strokes, breathing problems, increased health risk in childbirth, and psychological disorders.

Results or Consequences of Gluttony

In addition to the above health problems, there are three things that are direct results of gluttony:

- It is the fruit of selfishness, lack of self-control, and an undisciplined lifestyle.
- It brings on financial ruin (Prov. 23:20–21). Why? Because it brings on laziness (slothfulness).
- Spiritual ruin will also come from committing gluttony (Rom. 12:1–2), because the physical will override the spiritual.

The body must be used in God's service, so we are not free to expand the belly and bring harm and destruction to ourselves.

QUESTIONS

1. _____ is a sin and a lack of _____ _____.
2. Gluttony was a sin that concerned the early _____.
3. Gluttony has become one of the "accepted" _____ of our time.
4. Three of the reasons for Rome's fall were _____, _____ and _____.
5. Brethren, let's face it, in our _____ and _____ _____ society, we have a big problem on our hands!
6. Paul said to be _____ in all things.
7. Gluttony is the _____ desire of the sense of taste.
8. Gluttony is to eat to the _____, _____, squander or _____.
9. The _____, lazy _____ must bring himself under control.
10. The body must be used in _____ service and not just to expand the _____ and bring harm and _____ to it.

TRUE OR FALSE

1. ____ It matters what and how much one puts in the body.
2. ____ According to Philippians 3:18–19, the belly can become a god.
3. ____ Overeating and being "hoggish" has nothing to do with gluttony.
4. ____ Temperance (self-control) is the opposite virtue of gluttony.
5. ____ The word *breakfast* means to _____ your fast.

FIVE SIMPLE QUESTIONS

1. What verse in Habakkuk tells us not to sin against our own soul?
2. What verse in Titus says some in Paul's day were "dull, heavy, and lazy"?
3. What is the basic definition of gluttony?
4. Gluttony was one of the fundamental practices of what group of people in Acts 17?
5. What verses in Mark ask what would one give in exchange for his soul?

52

Plain Bible Talk

ABOUT MEMBERS OF THE CHURCH OF CHRIST

PURPOSE
To present twenty-six reasons I am a member of this "great" congregation.

GOAL
To encourage every member to love, defend, promote, and support the church.

CHALLENGING THOUGHT
The sign out front really says, "God's people worship here!"

KEY WORDS

church	servants	brethren
Bible	God	Christ
love	unity	souls
eternity		

CHOICES BEFORE US
Either we will live, act, dress, talk, and worship like God's people, or we will be just another religious group on earth! Read Zechariah 8:23.

THREE GREAT LESSONS
Faithful congregations respect the name of God.
Faithful congregations respect the people of God.
Faithful congregations respect the Word of God.

SCRIPTURES TO BE READ AND STUDIED

Acts 2:38, 47   Acts 28:15; 20:32
Matthew 16:18   Romans 16:16
Psalm 133:1

PRAYER FOR TODAY

Dear God, with all my being, I thank Thee for Thy grace, mercy, and love that allows me the great privilege of being a member of the church of Christ.

Introduction

I am blessed to be a member of the church of Christ. I hope and pray that every member shares the same love and respect for the local congregation that I do. Its members are not perfect, and there are things we certainly can improve upon, but I want to list some reasons I am a member of this congregation. A Frenchman once said, "America was great because the people were great." Thus I state that this congregation is a great congregation because we have great people! I sincerely pray that our young folks recognize this and also realize that godly men and women of the past laid the foundation for the good congregation we now have. These brethren stood on and for truth; they refused to compromise.

Twenty-Six Reasons I Am a Member of This Congregation

A. *Association* with some of the best people who have walked the earth (1 John 1:3).

B. *Baptism* is preached, practiced, and promoted (Mark 16:16).

C. *Church of Christ* is found in the Bible (Rom. 16:16).

D. *Dedication* to keep pure the church for the next generation (2 Cor. 11:2).

E. *Exalting Christ* and pointing folks to Calvary are priorities (1 Cor. 15:1–4).

F. *Father* is what we are privileged to call God. Only Christians can do so (Matt. 6:9).

G. *Good people* do good works to accomplish our mission (Tit. 3:1; Heb. 10:24).

H. *Heaven* is our prepared eternal home (John 14:1–3).

I. *Indescribable boldness* is exhibited as we "hold hands" and stand on truth (Eph. 6:13–20).

J. *Jesus* is magnified as our Savior, Friend, Master, and King (Phil. 1:20).

K. *Kind of church* the world and brethren need is found here (1 Thess. 1:3).

L. *Love* exists, is stated, and is shown here. We share joy and divide sorrow! (John 13:34–35).

M. *Mirrors, mouths, magnifiers, and ministers for God* are what members are (Isa. 6:8).

N. *Not a denomination* are we. We are New Testament Christians (Acts 2:38, 47; 11:26).

O. *Object of our faith* is the blood-stained cross (Rom. 3:25).

P. *Preachers* who preach the word are found in the pulpit (2 Tim. 4:2).

Q. *Qualified elders* lead, feed, and protect this flock (1 Tim. 3:1–7; Acts 20:28).

R. *Respect for God's name, book, and people* is practiced (Ps. 119:6).

S. *Serving deacons* are found here (1 Tim. 3:8–13).

T. *Teachers* instruct our children in the ways of God. Thank you! (2 Tim. 2:2).

U. *Unique unity* that exists in supporting good works (Ps. 133:1; Phil. 4:17–20).

V. *Victory in Jesus* is our goal and motto (Rev. 2:10; 14:13; Matt. 25:21).

W. *Women who are godly,* dedicated, and faithful ladies (Luke 10:42; John 19:25).

X. *"Xtra" miles* many go to make the church function smoothly (Luke 17:10; Matt. 5:41).

Y. *Young people* who will point the next generation to the pattern (Josh. 22:27–28).

Z. *Zest* (enjoyment, relish, enhancing) we have for worship and fellowship (Ps. 122:1).